To my beloved parents,
Dave and Suku Rendall,
who first taught me to hope

watching for the morning

VANEETHA RENDALL RISNER

watching for the morning

90 DEVOTIONALS FOR WHEN HOPE IS HARD TO FIND

PUBLISHING®
BRENTWOOD, TENNESSEE

979-8-3845-0015-5

Published by B&H Publishing Group
Brentwood, Tennessee

Dewey Decimal Classification: 242.4
Subject Heading: DEVOTIONAL LITERATURE / SUFFERING /
JOY AND SORROW

Cover design by Lindy Kasler. Cover images by Neil Warburton/
Stocksy and StockEU and colorful freedom/Shutterstock.
Author photo by Melanie Wasko.

1 2 3 4 5 6 • 28 27 26 25

Acknowledgments

So many people have touched my life, and their stories are reflected in these pages. I wish I could list all of them by name because their faith and friendship have shaped me. Since space is limited, I'm just mentioning a few, but know that this list of acknowledgments in no way represents all those I feel indebted to.

Mary, my wonderful editor, and the entire team at B&H, thank you for encouraging me to write this devotional and for cheering me on along the way.

Austin, I couldn't ask for a better agent, and I so appreciate all you do.

Margot, I'm so grateful for your terrific advice and input.

Aly and Jenny, it's a privilege working with you. One day I'll figure out how to post on social media.

Mom and Dad, you love me so well and have always supported me. Mom, you've faithfully modeled reading Scripture first thing in the morning, and that habit has shaped my life. Dad, you've always been a constant, and I know I can count on you for anything.

Ashley and Emily, it's a joy having you as bonus daughters. I'm so glad we're family—you're a wonderful part of my life.

Katie and Kristi, I treasure our biweekly Starbucks conversations, getting fashion critiques on the regular, and seeing Jesus in both of you. I couldn't have asked for better daughters or friends.

Shalini, you're my favorite sister and have always been my rock. There is no way this book would even exist without your help. I don't know how you managed to squeeze in twenty-five extra hours at the last minute, but somehow you did.

Joel, you are a dream come true, and I still can't believe I get to do life with you. There is no one in the world who has sacrificed more for me than you have, and no one has made me feel more loved.

Jesus, thank you for choosing me, saving me, and the breathtaking way you love me. I'm so grateful that I'll never have a single second without you.

Contents

Introduction

This book has been years in the making. It's a collection of my thoughts on suffering from experiences decades ago and some articles written many years ago when my world turned upside down. I wrote to remind myself of what I knew to be true, to give me hope as I was watching for the morning. Suffering has been a companion, mostly unwelcome, through the years. I contracted polio as an infant, was bullied because of my disability, endured four miscarriages, buried an infant son Paul, was diagnosed with post-polio syndrome (which may result in quadriplegia), went through an unwanted divorce, and struggled with single-parenting two adolescent daughters. But since much of that pain is behind me, as I began this devotional, I assumed most of the reflections would be captured from past experiences, while I was comfortably sitting in the pain-free present.

But God had different plans for me. He knew I needed to experience and live what I was writing so I wouldn't offer an academic view of pain but rather a real-time, in-the-trenches view. These last twelve months I've struggled with tremendous physical pain and losses, at times unable to think or write. So this book has become a compilation of both my past experiences and my all-too-real present.

God has been near. Closer than I could ask for. I've begged for more strength to finish this book, but God keeps reminding me that His grace is sufficient for me and His power is being made perfect in my weakness. I'm seeing signs of God's grace through my amazing sister, who actually *asked* if she could help edit and organize before either of us knew how physically difficult this month would be. My sister felt called to clear her schedule though she didn't know why. But God knew.

I don't know where you are today, but God does. He may feel distant, and you may be struggling to hold on to hope. When I'm in that place, I cling to the Word of God. That's why I have sprinkled fifteen memory verses throughout this devotional. If you do nothing else, I would love for you to commit these to memory. They will give you sturdy words to pray and promises to hold onto as you watch for the morning.

Today I read these words from Charles Spurgeon: "If there's anything in this world for which I would bless him more than anything else, it is for pain and affliction. I am sure that in these things the richest, most tender love has been manifested toward me. Love letters from heaven are often in black-edged envelopes. The cloud that is black with horror is big with mercy."[1] I think Spurgeon would agree with me when I say, "The cloud that seems black with horror is *in reality* big with mercy."

I pray that the Lord will meet you in these pages, and that you will discover that the black-edged envelopes in your life contain love letters from God.

1

Beauty in the Broken

Now we have this treasure in clay jars,
so that this extraordinary power may
be from God and not from us.
2 CORINTHIANS 4:7

Kintsugi reminds us there is beauty in the broken. It is a Japanese art that repairs broken pottery with gold, rendering a new piece that is more exquisite than it was before the break. It literally means "to join with gold."

Rather than trying to hide the damage, kintsugi highlights the repair. The imperfections make it beautiful and valuable. A broken piece that is put back together has more of a story, seems more authentic and real, and is stronger and more resilient than something that has stayed pristine. The breaking of what once was, the layered and time-consuming process of putting it back together, the mending it with gold—all contribute to its value. And surprisingly, it becomes more resilient after it has been mended by kintsugi, even stronger than it was before.

God is the Restorer, the kintsugi Master who skillfully and tenderly puts the broken pieces of our lives back together. It takes time, but God leaves no broken piece untouched. I think of the gold resin as the work and power of God, who redeems what is broken in our lives.

Jay Wolf says, "The story of kintsugi may be the most perfect embodiment of all our trauma-shattered lives. . . . Instead of throwing away the broken beloved pottery, we'll fix it in a way that doesn't pretend it hasn't been broken but honors the breaking—and more so, the surviving—by highlighting those repaired seams with gold lacquer."[2]

After reading about this art, I decided to make my own kintsugi vase since the authentic ones were expensive. Besides, I wouldn't mind breaking a dish for the cause. I found some do-it-yourself instructions online about how to make faux kintsugi, particularly how to break it cleanly, and laughed as one man observed that deliberately breaking pottery just to put it back together defeated the real meaning behind kintsugi. He wasn't wrong but I forged ahead.

A friend came over and helped me with the process. Ironically, I wanted my bowl to look perfect and wasted hours trying to make it look clean and authentic. Kintsugi is about embracing and honoring flaws, but apparently, I like curated imperfections.

As I stared at the piece on my shelf, I mourned what was broken in my life. I was once an artist, expressing myself through graphic art, and now I needed help even with this relatively simple project because of the limits my body held.

Then I saw it. The way God was blessing my increasingly broken body. My writing came from a desire to express myself, which could no longer be through graphic art. I realized that God, the master Artist, was putting my life back together with the gold of His presence and grace to show that the extraordinary power belongs to Him and not to me. He is doing a work in my life and yours that is beyond our understanding.

Our lives are in God's hands, and He is using our brokenness to create something beautiful.

REFLECT: Where has your life been broken? How have you seen the master Artist bless you, and others, through those gold-lined, once-broken places?

Responding to Suffering

Therefore, submit to God. Resist the devil,
and he will flee from you. Draw near to
God, and he will draw near to you.
JAMES 4:7–8

When I'm struggling, my thoughts are all over the place. I can seamlessly go from anger to despair to doubt, and before I know it, I'm in the pit. I keep spiraling downward until I stop and refocus, turning to God, remembering and rehearsing the truths I need to hold onto. Passages like this one in James 4 help me reorient my heart.

Verse 7 begins with "therefore," connecting this call to what comes before it: a reminder of God's favor toward the humble, to those who have chosen friendship with God rather than with the world. When I approach God humbly, He draws near, pulling me even closer to Him and further away from the prideful ways of the world.

The posture I bring is important. When I submit to God, I'm acknowledging that He is sovereign over my life. I need His Spirit who lives in me, cultivating the humility we're called to have, and offering His grace to make it through suffering. Submitting in suffering reorients my mind to God and to my utter dependence on Him. It is trusting Him with the outcome, knowing He will give me what is best.

"Resist the devil, and he will flee from you." Before I can resist the devil, I need to be aware of his schemes. Throughout Scripture we see that Satan wants us to believe that God isn't for us, that God doesn't care, and that God isn't good. Satan wants us to be self-reliant, to assume we don't need God or His wisdom, and to believe instead that we are better off without God. Satan, the accuser, wants us to feel accused, guilty, desperate, and hopeless. So when those thoughts start creeping in, I need to recognize they may be the work of the devil.

The best way I know to resist the devil is to repeat Scripture, just as Jesus did. And if I have verses at my fingertips, committed to memory, I can draw them out when the devil prowls around. I can call on Jesus and ask Him for help and deliverance from all my fears.

Then I deliberately draw near to God. I turn toward Him. It's not that He meets me halfway. I just turn around and He does the rest. He is always waiting, always with me, always willing. But as I turn around to face Him, I know He is there.

We all need to fight for faith when we're suffering. And if you don't recognize the battle, you will go in unarmed. You may succumb to your fears, framing and reframing your circumstances in light of your feelings rather than the truths you know about God. So perhaps this is a good first verse to memorize. In our despair, we need words to cry out instinctively, words that shape our minds and our responses.

MEMORIZE: Write today's verse on an index card. Put it where you'll see it regularly so you can memorize it.

3

Does God Feel Cruel?

He did not even spare his own Son but
gave him up for us all. How will he not
also with him grant us everything?
ROMANS 8:32

Not too long ago, I overheard my daughter Kristi say on the phone, "Sometimes I think God is low-key savage. It seems like He wants to take away the things we don't even realize we rely on." I was taken aback. God? Low-key savage? Kristi had to explain the meaning to me: subtly ruthless with a touch of irony.

Then I realized many of us suspect that, but we phrase it differently. A friend shared at Bible study, "I have lots of fears, particularly about my family's safety. I'm afraid to ask God to help me get over them because I don't know what He'll do." We laughed because we can all relate.

Yet I know that God isn't cruel or unkind, despite how it looks. Everything He brings into our life, including trials, is out of love, to do us good in the end.

When I was two, I couldn't walk but was happy to be carried around on people's shoulders. So when I woke up with my legs in a cast after my first surgery, I wondered why I was in so much pain and why I couldn't move my legs. I was furious at my mother and then broke down in tears, promising not to be naughty if she would take away the horrible white pajamas.

I thought I was being punished. And even after my mother tried to explain it to me, I didn't understand. How could I grasp that this surgery could one day help me walk? I couldn't. In my two-year-old mind, I just wanted to go back to the way things were. My mother bravely watched me suffer, knowing I blamed her for my pain. She hated seeing me in pain, and if there was another way to help me walk, she would have done it.

In the same way, God does not enjoy seeing us suffer. He loves us more than an earthly parent ever could.

When I asked Kristi about her conversation, she said, "I know God isn't savage. But I told my friend sometimes it *feels* like that because He knows what motivates us and takes away the things we rely on. But I learned that when God takes things away, it makes us rely on Him more, which in the end is so much better."

She's right. Life circumstances can make us *feel* like God is being cruel. Maybe you feel that way today because God has taken away something or someone that was precious to you. Despite how you feel, know that God loves you and everything you experience comes from that love. He who didn't spare His son because He loves us that much wants to give you everything good. You can trust Him.

If you are tempted to doubt the Lord's intentions, these words from Charles Spurgeon may comfort you as they have me: "Affliction does not come haphazardly, the weight of every stroke is accurately measured . . . the knife of the heavenly Surgeon never cuts deeper than is absolutely necessary."[3]

REFLECT: Where, in your own life, have you suspected God of being "low-key savage"? How have you learned to rely more on God in the losses you've endured?

4

God Is in All Things

Your judgments stand firm today, for
all things are your servants.

PSALM 119:91

R ecently I was hurt by a friend's insensitive comment. My
first response was irritation, and then I began mentally
cataloging a list of grievances—remembering all the other times
I'd been hurt by her.

It might have ended there, but when I came across these
words from A. W. Tozer, I started thinking differently about the
situation: "If we understand that everything happening to us is
to make us more Christlike, it will solve a great deal of anxiety
in our lives."[4]

Everything that is happening to me is to make me more
Christlike. Nothing is excluded. Joy and pain. Suffering and
ease. People who love me and people who hurt me.

I stopped focusing on my friend's comment and wondered
why God might have brought this situation into my life. It was

a simple question, but the answers revealed more about my heart than hers. My friend's actions were an avenue for God to reveal a layer of sin in my life that I otherwise would have glossed over. As I saw the sin in my response, I was able to confess it to God and repent.

Whenever I feel annoyed or frustrated or angry, perhaps God is inviting me to examine my own heart instead of focusing my attention outward. Perhaps my irritation is an invitation from the Lord to go deeper with Him. God may be doing something far more important and more lasting in me than what is happening to me.

No experience is ever wasted. My difficult circumstances can cultivate a dependence on Christ and teach me to pray more fervently. And my successes can lead me to praise God and give Him glory. And perhaps teach me humility by taking the low seat even in the limelight. Everything can be a stepping stone to holiness.

Madame Guyon had a difficult life, marked by illness, neglect, and humiliation. When she was sixteen, her father tricked her into marrying a man who was twenty-two years older and afflicted with gout. Guyon became his nurse and cared for him tirelessly, living in her mother-in-law's home, even after she spread vicious lies about her.

Guyon deeply trusted God's character and saw that her father's deceit and mother-in-law's lies were both blessings because they enabled her to humbly turn to God and see His great love for her.[5] Rather than growing bitter at the pain she'd endured, she chose to see God's loving hand in it—that God had brought all her circumstances to draw her closer to Him.

Everything that is difficult in our lives is a divine invitation to turn to God. Our annoyances can reveal our sin. People who hurt us give us opportunities to forgive. Our physical ailments teach us to depend on God.

Everything that happens to us can make us more like Christ.

————————

PRAY: Heavenly Father, turn my eyes from what is outside of me to what is inside of me. Meet me in that place. Reveal what is in my heart, and make me more like You.

The Gift of Psalm 139

LORD, you have searched me and known me.

PSALM 139:1

I memorized Scripture for years because people said that's what Christians do. I began memorizing lengthy passages in college, proud that I knew them, but never connecting them to my everyday life. In fact, I didn't use them for anything. Since I could easily find verses in my Bible, I wondered why people were so hung up on committing long passages to memory.

That is, until I walked into Maria's psych ward. She felt broken and wondered if she'd ever think clearly again. And she wondered where God was in all of this. I had seen her spiral downward for days but didn't know what was happening until she told me she was diagnosed with bipolar disorder.

She was thankful to see me, admitting everything was still so overwhelming to her, and she couldn't understand herself or her actions.

I wasn't sure what to say or pray. Since I'd memorized Psalm 139, it came to me as I sat with her and I started putting her name into the verses. I began "You have searched Maria, and you know her. You know when Maria sits and when she rises. You perceive Maria's thoughts from afar. You know when Maria is going out and when she is lying down; you are familiar with all her ways. Before a word is on Maria's tongue, you know it completely" (Ps. 139:1–4 NIV, author's paraphrase).

Maria was gripped by these words. This was hope to hold onto. When I finished the psalm, Maria and I were both emotional. God knew what had happened and knew Maria better than she knew herself. He knew every thought she's had and every word she'd uttered. And He was with her in her confusion.

Maria later told me that hearing Psalm 139 with her name in it was game-changing. It altered how she viewed her situation. God was in the psych ward with her, even though she felt alone. God was there when her brain was going in a million directions. And God would always be there for her, no matter where she was. She saw that she was fearfully and wonderfully made by Him; God had not made a mistake in her design.

I realized then how much more powerful God's words were than mine to comfort others. When we memorize Scripture, we offer the comfort of God—words that speak directly and individually to each person. The Scripture I've memorized has given me comfort and encouragement, words to pray and promises to cling to, for myself and for others when we need gospel hope.

If memorizing Scripture feels boring to you, perhaps you can begin by asking God what to memorize—which passages to hide in your heart so they will be there when you need them.

———————

PRACTICE: Open your Bible to Psalm 139 and read it aloud, personalizing every verse.

6

When the Detour Becomes the New Road

I will lead the blind by a way they did not know;
I will guide them on paths they have not known.
I will turn darkness to light in front of them
and rough places into level ground.
This is what I will do for them,
and I will not abandon them.

ISAIAH 42:16

*T*his isn't the ticket I bought.

That's what I thought when I first started noticing weakness in my arm, and I found myself on a road I hadn't anticipated. A road I wasn't prepared for. A road I didn't want to travel.

Laura Story understands how that feels. Her world radically changed after her husband Martin was diagnosed with a brain tumor. As she watched him struggle with devastating memory loss, Laura begged God to heal Martin and restore their lives to the way they were. Life hadn't been perfect, but it had been good.

Looking back, Laura reflected, "What we thought was the detour in our life after realizing things weren't going back to normal, was actually the road."[6]

The detour is actually the road. That sounds horrifying. When my plans go awry, I always want to believe that I have taken a temporary detour. Maybe it's a long one, but I hope that the real road, the road where I can return to being happy and fulfilled, is just ahead. Maybe it's only around the corner if I can simply hang on.

I wonder how to pray: Should I earnestly ask God to change my circumstances? Should I draw near to Him in prayer, write down my requests, and regularly seek Him for the things in my life I want to see changed?

Or do I recognize that I'm on a different road? One that may not bring the healing and restoration I would like but rather a closeness to Jesus I could not get any other way. Do I hold loosely to the expectation of changed circumstances and cling tighter to the hope that will never disappoint—the hope that is rooted in Jesus?

Yes.

God invites me to ask Him to change the things I long to be different. To trust that my prayers make a difference.

At the same time, God bids me to accept where I am. To let Him meet me in the darkness. To find comfort in His presence. To see Him as more important than any change in my circumstances.

God calls me to do both. Every day. On every road.

I cannot cling to the past. I cannot get back on the old road and put everything back the way it was. Some things will get better over time. Some prayers will be miraculously answered. Some dreams will come true. But the old road is gone.

This new road I am on, bumpy and twisty as it may be, is the path God has chosen for me. I know He is here. This road is the only one worth taking.

WRITE: Write down the path your life has taken in the form of a brief timeline. Then invite God to show you the ways He has sustained and supported you at each twist and turn. Listen. Capture where you see God's kind provision even when what seemed to be a detour was the road.

What If the Worst Happens?

"If the God we serve exists, then he can rescue us from the furnace of blazing fire, and he can rescue us from the power of you, the king. But even if he does not rescue us, we want you as king to know that we will not serve your gods or worship the gold statue you set up."

DANIEL 3:17–18

Years ago, I found myself growing fearful. Not a heart-stopping, all-encompassing fear but the kind of constant gnawing that occurs when you look at the discouraging trends of the present and assume things will never change. When you think about the future and wonder, *What if the worst happens?*

We all face a staggering array of what-ifs. Some are minor, while others have life-altering repercussions. What if my child dies? What if I get cancer? What if my spouse leaves me?

The uncomfortable truth is that any of those things could happen. No one is free from tragedy or pain. None of us are guaranteed an easy life.

While struggling with singleness brought about by unwanted divorce, rebellious adolescents, and a weakening body, I imagined the worst happening in every situation. I wondered, *What if my inmost longings are never met and my nightmares come true?* I sat poring over my Bible, asking these questions and others I'd wrestled with for decades. "Is God enough? If my deepest fears are realized, will God still be sufficient?"

I wondered: *If my children rebel and never walk closely with the Lord, will God be enough? If I never remarry and never feel loved by a man again, will God be enough? If my suffering continues and I never see the purpose in it, will God be enough?* I wish I automatically said, "Yes, of course God will be sufficient." But I didn't want to give up my dreams, surrender those things that were dear to me, relinquish what I felt entitled to.

I reluctantly opened my hands, filled with my dreams, and surrendered them to Him. I wanted to love God for who He is and not for and not for what I wanted from Him.

God's presence overwhelmed me as He reminded me that I have something far better than a reassurance that my dreaded what-ifs won't happen. I have the assurance that even if they do happen, He will be there in the midst of them. He will carry me and comfort me. God doesn't promise me a trouble-free life, but He does promise never to leave me.

Before Shadrach, Meshach, and Abednego were thrown into the fire, they offered some of the most courageous words ever spoken. "If we are thrown into the blazing furnace, the God we serve is able to deliver us. . . . But even if he does not, we want you to know . . . that we will not serve your gods" (Dan. 3:17–18 NIV).

Even if the worst happens, God's grace will be sufficient.

Replacing "what if" with "even if" is one of the most liberating exchanges we can ever make. We trade our irrational fears of an uncertain future for the loving assurance of an unchanging God. We see that even if the worst happens, God will carry us. He will still be good. And He will never leave us.

———————

REFLECT: What concerns or fears are you carrying? What shifts in you when you move from what-if fears to even-if prayers?

8

Will God Really Provide All I Need?

And my God will supply every need of yours
according to his riches in glory in Christ Jesus.
PHILIPPIANS 4:19 RSV

Several years ago, we built our home and made sure it was completely wheelchair accessible. While I often use a wheelchair now and I'm grateful for that provision, I don't like wheelchairs. They represent limitations and loss.

This isn't the kind of provision I want. I want healing and wholeness. A body that doesn't tire easily and the ability to do whatever I choose. I want freedom and independence. But God had something else in mind.

During our move, I had help with packing and unpacking but felt embarrassed to have others see into my closets and dresser drawers. I had five long-sleeved white shirts in my closet (a fashion staple), six boxes of storage bags in my pantry (they were a bargain), and a can of bug spray in every room (Doesn't everyone have that?).

I wanted to present my best self, but as people packed and unpacked everything in my life, I had no secrets. I wanted to say, "Leave that. I'll do it myself," but I couldn't. My life was laid bare.

While this struggle felt intensely personal and unique to me, I know it is not. Not everyone struggles with physical limitations, but everyone has limitations.

Some days I know God is providing for all my needs. But other days, when I am faced with unexpected new weakness or pain, I doubt. As I look at a future that is headed in a seemingly irreversible direction, I wonder if God will truly provide.

When I spiral downward, increasingly agitated about the future, God ever so gently reminds me of the truth. His word speaks directly to each of my fears.

My fear: My arms will grow so weak I can't feed myself.

God's response: "Do not be anxious about your life. . . . Consider the ravens: they neither sow nor reap, they have neither storehouse nor barn, and yet God feeds them" (Luke 12:22, 24 RSV).

My fear: I won't have fun or enjoy life.

God's response: "In your presence there is fullness of joy; at your right hand are pleasures forevermore" (Ps. 16:11 ESV).

My fear: People will think less of me when they see my bad habits.

God's response: "The fear of human opinion disables; trusting in GOD protects you from that" (Prov. 29:25 MSG).

When I anchor my life on truth, I am filled with faith. Faith in what I know to be true, despite what I see before me. There is no need to despair.

With these truths, I see my house as God's abundant provision for me. No matter what the future holds, God will go with me. He is all I need, and I will lack no good thing.

———————

MEMORIZE: Write today's verse on an index card. Put it where you'll see it regularly so you can memorize it.

9

Watching for the Morning

I wait for the LORD; I wait and put my hope in his word. I wait for the Lord more than watchmen for the morning—more than watchmen for the morning.
PSALM 130:5–6

Waiting for the Lord.

Hoping in His Word.

Watching for the morning.

Those phrases from Psalm 130 still bring me to tears. They describe how I lived for years, after my once-comfortable life dissolved in front of me. My husband had left, and my world was falling apart. I waited, hoped, and watched for life to be good again.

I wanted the wait to be over so my life could return to normal. But those years taught me that in God's hands, waiting is not an empty space to be rushed past. Waiting has a purpose, much more refining than I ever imagined.

The psalms showed me how to wait. I read them over and over. They taught me how to trust God even in my darkest hours. They named the ache in my waiting and gave me words I could offer to God. I learned that waiting is a holy exercise, one that requires my full attention. I wanted to be busy while I waited, to distract myself from the pain of the present empty moment and my overwhelming longings, but God invited me to bring those longings to Him instead.

Still, in my impatience I wanted to move on and move past my pain. If impatience is being discontent with the present moment, then patience is embracing the present and letting God meet me in it.

At first, I simply wanted an indication that my prayers would be answered. Was life going to get better, or would it continue to deteriorate? Would I get what I'd prayed for, or would God's answer be no? I wanted to know which outcome to put my hope in.

Yet the psalms also showed me that God was deepening my faith in my waiting. That's when I learned that my hope wasn't in an outcome. It was in God alone. I wasn't watching and waiting for the morning; I was watching and waiting for God. The night was still pitch-black as I learned to wait for God more watchfully than watchmen wait for the morning. I realized that the night is darkest just before morning. As the sun rises, watchmen see shadows dimly in the receding darkness that become clearer as the night turns into day. They are looking closely, and they have no doubt about the outcome.

The psalms are songs of hope. Not hope that our situation will change immediately but hope in the God who cares tenderly for us and has all of eternity to show us what He did in our waiting. Our hope is in Him (Ps. 39:7) and from Him (Ps. 62:5), and we wait patiently for Him (Ps. 37:7), more than watchmen wait for the morning.

———————

REFLECT: Consider your life right now. What feels most uncertain? What might God be doing in what appears to be an empty silence?

Grace for the Moment

"Do not fear, for I have redeemed you;
I have called you by your name; you are mine.
When you pass through the waters,
I will be with you."

ISAIAH 43:1–2

Several years ago, when I was worried about the future, a friend gave me an article about uncertainty that helped explain my angst.

In the article, a Michigan research team studied patients who had colostomies—some of whom knew their colostomy was permanent while others had the possibility of having it reversed. Six months later, the patients who knew their difficult condition was irreversible were happier than those who were still waiting to find out if they could return to normal.

The author asked, "Why would we prefer to know the worst than to suspect it?"[7] In other words, fearing a terrible event is worse than having it happen.

Uncertainty is paralyzing. We can't make plans. We don't know how to feel. We can't make peace with the outcome because we don't know what it is. We must live in limbo, which can be the hardest place to rest.

Thinking about a difficult future makes me uneasy and anxious. I've never lacked anything I've needed in the moment, yet I'm irrationally afraid that I won't have what I need in the future.

This fear isn't easy to overcome since it is illogical. It isn't based on fact. Or history. Or evidence of any kind. But it's real nonetheless. I've realized that I need to trust that God will give me the grace I need in the moment I need it.

I can't imagine it now because I can't go to the future. A friend who is battling cancer recently said, "I'm not afraid of death because I know where I will go, but I am afraid of dying." Most of us can relate to this statement; we wonder how we will face dying.

Ed Welch, the author of *Running Scared*, insightfully offers:

> Among my assorted fears and anxieties is the fear of suffocation, especially through drowning. . . . What does tomorrow's manna, future grace, have to do with such fears? It doesn't say that I will be spared suffocation. . . .
>
> If I am called to drown, I don't know what grace I will receive. Having never had it, I can't imagine it, and since God gives much more than we ask, my prediction no doubt would fall far short. It is enough to know that I will receive

grace. I will know the presence of the Spirit and I will die, or be rescued, in a way that pleases the Lord.[8]

I'm trusting that God will give me the grace I need when I need it. Can you trust Him for that today too?

PRAY: Father, I don't know the future, but I know that every moment of my life—past, present, and future—is in Your hands. You will always give me the grace I need. In life and in death, I belong to You. Thank You for Your unfailing, never-ending, steadfast love.

Believing God Has
a Purpose

We know that all things work together
for the good of those who love God, who
are called according to his purpose.
Romans 8:28

I have a love/hate relationship with Romans 8:28. I struggle with the part that reads "all things work together for the good" because I've been hammered with it more than once. A man quoted it at my son's funeral, as he shook my hand standing in line, assuring me that God was using Paul's death for good. That day I needed comfort and tears, not theology. People have mentioned that verse at other times as well when they want to avoid the messiness of my present pain by looking to a future purpose.

Yet Romans 8:28 has been a life-giving verse to me because it has reassured me that God has a purpose in all my suffering.

Nothing can thwart His good plans for me. Everything I go through is working for my good because God makes no mistakes.

I first heard about this idea just before Paul died. Before that, I assumed God loved me but hadn't considered *everything* as part of God's plan. It seemed there was too much pain in the lives of other Christians, and in my life, to believe God was working it all for our good.

Reading the following words was at first shocking and then life-changing for me. They came from Evelyn Christenson, a woman who had three miscarriages, a stillborn baby, and an infant who died at seven months. She said, "This is the place you reach when after years and years of trials and difficulties, you see that all has been working out for your good, and that God's will is perfect. You see that He has made no mistakes. He knew all of the 'what if's' in your life. When you finally recognize this, even during the trials, it's possible to have joy, deep down joy."[9]

Those words made no sense to me when I first read them and felt impossible right after Paul's death, but now after seeing years of God's faithfulness, I can echo that God has made no mistakes. And even when I cannot understand why, I can trust that He has a purpose. There is always a reason, maybe thousands of them. As John Piper said, "God is always doing 10,000 things in your life, and you may be aware of three of them."[10]

This idea of purpose is woven throughout Scripture. Joseph told his brothers after they betrayed him, "You planned evil against me; God planned it for good" (Gen. 50:20). Paul recognized that his thorn in the flesh was a messenger from Satan to torment him, yet God used it to make Paul even more effective in his ministry (2 Cor. 12:7–9). Satan wanted to destroy Job's faith, but the trials he brought ultimately strengthened Job (Job 42:10–17).

Nothing can happen to any of us who love Jesus that is not for our good. And one day in heaven, we will thank God for everything He has brought into our lives.

———————

REFLECT: Have you ever felt that God has made a mistake? Remember the details of that time. How does the idea of purpose land right now? If it feels impossible, don't pressure yourself to see a purpose. Ask God to hold you tenderly while you rest in His love.

12

A Look into My Personal Journal

Yet once more I will shake not only the earth but also the heavens. This expression, "Yet once more," indicates the removal of what can be shaken—that is, created things—so that what is not shaken might remain.

HEBREWS 12:26–27

My journal is a record of God's faithfulness. These are journal entries from three consecutive days.

Entry from December 19, 2023

Another day of exhaustion. Oh Lord, please help me. I've been sick for days on end. . . . I can't imagine what life was like before. . . . Now life has become so small.

I'm at the end of myself. Melanie said in thirty years she'd never heard me so weary. Thin. Overwhelmed.

Entry from December 20, 2023

Yesterday, I kept hearing these words echoing throughout the day, "Do you love me more than these?" It's from John 21:15, but it seems so out of context. Yet for me it also felt like a tender question—that perhaps the stripping away was an invitation from God—a way to delight in Him and make Him my treasure. Was it, Lord?

You've stripped away:

- Walking: I can't walk with this cyst on my spine.
- Strength: I'm getting weaker every day, canceling activities because I'm too tired to go even with Joel.
- Sleep: I can't sleep through the night because of the pain and can't turn myself in bed.
- Feeling well/alert: Covid is lingering and I'm always exhausted.
- My love of food: G.I. issues and I hate being gluten free and dairy free.
- Vanity: My hair falling out in handfuls. My thin hair makes me feel unattractive.
- Clothing: Finding moth holes in all my wool sweaters last week.
- The house: Termites under our garage! Pest people said worst termite damage they've seen in ten years.
- Friends: I can't leave the house to go meet them.

- Pain free: I live with pain in my shoulders, my hands, and my legs.

That list is awful and overwhelming, and yet, Lord, I do love You more than these. Please keep me from discouragement, or just waiting for it all to get better. I'm asking You to fix all these things in the name of Jesus. I am a child of the King. And as I wait for complete fulfillment, draw me close.

Entry from December 21, 2023

I keep pondering that question, "Do you love me more than these?" When I think that this has all been purposeful, that it has come from Your hand, I can accept it and even find joy in it. . . . You've called me to this. You are shaking what can be shaken so that what is unshakable remains.

[Then I turned to Haggai as part of my daily reading. I was trembling as I saw and wrote the following verse]: "Once more, in a little while, I am going to shake the heavens and the earth, the sea and the dry land" (Hag. 2:6).

I was stunned. My reference from Hebrews 12 came from the passage I'd just read in Haggai. This was undoubtedly God's message to me—that He was shaking what could be shaken, for my good, so that what was unshakable would remain.

WRITE: Record the events of the past week. What were your joys and difficulties? When did God seem absent? When did you experience His presence?

Are You Tired of Waiting?

"Now, Lord, what do I wait for?
My hope is in you."
PSALM 39:7

I want instant in my life. I love Venmo, microwaves, and Amazon same-day delivery. Waiting seems like a holdup, an empty place to bide my time before I receive what I want.

Even in the important things of life, I've grown impatient in my waiting: healing from a protracted illness, finding relief from pain and growing weakness, restoration of a relationship, and fulfillment of a deep longing.

Waiting is part of the human condition, and I take great comfort that people in the Bible experienced it and struggled through it, too. Even Abraham, with whom God initiated a covenant that would one day bring the Savior, grew impatient when his prayers didn't materialize as he had hoped.

When God promised Abraham that he would be the father of many nations, Abraham's wife, Sarah, was already barren and well past her childbearing years. After hearing nothing further about it for eleven long years, both Abraham and Sarah assumed they needed to help God's promise along. So Abraham took Hagar, Sarah's servant, who then gave birth to Ishmael. It seemed that God's promises could be fulfilled through Ishmael.

Abraham had figured out a way to have heirs on his own; he wanted God to work through what he'd already done. So he asked God to bless him through Ishmael (Gen. 17:18) rather than waiting for another son. Thirteen years later God told them Sarah would bear a son, Isaac.

Like Abraham, I want to know with certainty what's going to happen and then move ahead. Abraham wanted to have descendants through Ishmael rather than wait for what only God could do. But God had something different in mind.

Like Abraham, has your waiting turned into months, years, and even decades? Do you find yourself turning your heart away from God, who seemingly never delivered what you were waiting for? Like Abraham, are you setting your hopes on Ishmael—the thing you have control over, the thing that doesn't require waiting and trusting?

What is happening in our waiting? Is it just the empty space between our prayers and their fulfillment? No, in our waiting, God does His deepest work. Waiting is not passive. He is teaching us to trust Him. Our hope is in Him.

God has not forgotten you. Your requests are not unimportant. He sees what you cannot see; He knows the potential dangers and snares He is protecting you from, and His timing is always perfect.

It's easy to grow weary and take matters into our own hands because it's taking so long. It's tempting to look for Ishmael, to meet our desires our way. But don't short-circuit what God has for you. Don't settle for Ishmael when God has Isaac for you. Isaac was worth waiting for.

Don't settle for what is humanly possible; wait for what only God can do.

———————

REFLECT: What is your Ishmael? What are you waiting for? When are you tempted to stop waiting for by taking control yourself?

Do Not Fear

Do not fear, for I am with you;
do not be afraid, for I am your God.
I will strengthen you; I will help you;
I will hold on to you with my righteous right hand.

ISAIAH 41:10

One of my greatest fears is public speaking, and any group of more than five people counts. My husband can attest that almost every time I'm about to get on stage I say to him, "Why did I agree to do this?" I'm shaking and nervous, wishing I could be anywhere else. I'm afraid I'm going to forget all I've rehearsed and make a fool of myself on stage.

In that fear, I've learned to talk to myself, repeating Isaiah 41:10. The words here for "do not fear" and "do not be afraid" are different in Hebrew. The first means just normal fear, but the second one is related to looking around. The NASB1995 translates that verse: "Do not anxiously look about you." That's exactly what I do when I'm afraid. I look around at the people in the audience. I think about how talented other speakers are. I focus on the potential for something awful.

That's the essence of fear, isn't it? It's not what we are dealing with right now but the dread of what might happen. So those two commands are the things we need to keep telling ourselves. Don't be afraid. Don't look around anxiously. Don't focus on your fear but focus on God. The best way to drive out fear is to anchor yourself in the presence and promises of God.

I love these verses because I see them as God speaking directly to me. There are five reasons in this passage not to fear, which are the five most precious things I can imagine. First, that God is with me. I am not on stage by myself, trying to inspire the audience with my words.

Second, my God is the Maker of heaven and earth. The One who knows my heart and knows every word I speak before I say it. He created everyone in the audience and knows what they need.

Third, God will strengthen me. In my weakness God's power is being made perfect. I am stronger than my innate ability because I am serving in the strength God provides.

Fourth, God will help me. Even if I mess up and forget everything I wanted to say, God will help me. I don't need to frantically rehearse my words as much as I need to ask God to calm my fears.

Last, God will hold onto me. It's not up to me to get this right. I can relax, knowing that His strong arms are around me, even when I don't have the strength to hold onto Him.

These promises are for all of us. The God who spoke the world into existence tells us all not to fear. All we need to do is trust Him.

MEMORIZE: Write today's verse on an index card. Put it where you'll see it regularly so you can memorize it.

Dandelion Grace

*"Truly, truly, I say to you, unless a grain of
wheat falls into the earth and dies, it remains
alone; but if it dies, it bears much fruit."*
JOHN 12:24 (ESV)

Years ago, I helped organize our church's VBS and oversaw all the crafts. I spent hours finding ideas, cutting construction paper, and gathering all the supplies. I loved hearing parents' comments on what their children brought home. But I can't serve that way anymore; now I have to worry about even walking down the children's hall, afraid I could get knocked down. At times now I feel useless.

I know the Christian life isn't all about usefulness. I am not indispensable in the kingdom—none of us are. God delights in us, not because of anything we offer or accomplish but simply because we are His beloved children. This life is not about our glory—the impact we make on this world—but about God's glory. His grace is sufficient for us, and His power is made perfect in our weakness. When we look weak, we are often our strongest.

When I think about the contrast between being energetic and productive versus losing energy and strength, I picture the dying dandelion. In its heyday, the dandelion is bright and rugged. It grows in harsh conditions, often in places where no one sees or knows but God. Some people see it as unstoppable, its bright yellow petals visible from a distance. Their noticeable color attracts and feeds the bees, and their spreading softens hard and compacted soil to enable other plants to thrive.

But as it is dying, stripped of its strength, the dandelion is often hard to see. It has given everything, and there seems to be nothing left; the vibrant color that once defined it is gone. In this stage it is preparing to reproduce, doing its most glorious work. This is what captivates me about the dandelion—its delicate beauty and far-reaching influence at the end of its life. That is when it brings life to others.

We often feel most useful to God when we are sunny, strong, and resilient. People notice us. But when our health changes and we feel delicate and dependent, we wonder what good our lives are. And society reinforces that doubt by ignoring the elderly, shunning the disabled, aborting the unwanted. It's almost as if we must prove our usefulness for society to value us. When we aren't accomplishing anything visible to others, we may feel like a burden, wishing we could serve rather than be served.

But when does the dandelion do its most important work? When it's dying. When the fragile seeds are blown away by the wind. When it has surrendered itself and is sowing seeds of new life. And the stronger the wind blows, the farther the seeds will go—to places that one lone flower could never have gone itself.

REFLECT: How have you measured your worth by your personal strengths and accomplishments? What do you need to surrender to God in your weakness? What would that look like?

16

Shattered Dreams
and Shaken Faith

"Are you the one who is to come, or
shall we look for another?"
<small>MATTHEW 11:3 ESV</small>

Shattered dreams can shake our faith. It's easy to question what we have long believed. We wonder what is real, especially when experience doesn't match expectations.

This wavering troubles me. I, who have enjoyed close fellowship with God, have no answers in my disappointment and pain.

John the Baptist understood this struggle as he waited in prison. He knew who Jesus was. He baptized Jesus and saw God's Spirit descend on Him, testifying that He indeed was the Son of God.

And yet, at the height of Jesus's ministry, John had the courage to send word to Him from prison, asking, "Are you the one who is to come, or shall we look for another?" (Matt. 11:3 ESV).

At one point, John was sure Jesus was the Messiah. When John baptized Jesus, he heard a voice from heaven declare, "This is my beloved Son, with whom I am well-pleased" (Matt. 3:17). Jesus further confirmed His divinity by performing miracles, yet now John was wondering what was true.

Why?

John knew from Scripture that He who gave the blind sight and made the lame walk could surely open "the prison to those who are bound" as prophesied in Isaiah 61:1 (ESV). But Jesus didn't do that for John.

So perhaps at this point, John doubted what he knew. If Jesus was indeed the Messiah, John probably expected to have a role in His earthly kingdom. He wouldn't have expected to start with such a high calling, only to end his life and his ministry in a prison cell. None of those expectations coincided with reality. And that may have caused John to doubt. Unfulfilled expectations often elicit that response in me.

Jesus didn't condemn John for his doubts. He even said that no one greater than John has ever lived. He understood why John was asking the question. But John had to accept Christ's plans for his life. Plans that were different from what he envisioned. He had to dwell on what he knew to be true rather than draw conclusions based on his circumstances.

Like John, God calls me to trust what I know to be true from Scripture and from experience, that God is wise and loving and completely sovereign.

When your plans crumble, you can trust in God's infinite wisdom. When your suffering seems too much to bear, you can rest in His compassionate love. When your life spins out of control, you can rely on God's absolute sovereignty.

Even when you don't understand what's happening, don't stop talking to Him or turn away in fear. Go to Jesus and tell Him your doubts. John's doubts were similar to yours. You may wonder if God is who He says He is and if everything is under His control and if He truly loves you. He is and He does.

Will you trust in your circumstances that constantly change? Or will you trust God who is unchanging?

———————

PRAY: Lord, right now I am struggling to understand Your ways especially in _____. I know You are loving, wise, sovereign, but help me trust what I know to be true. All my hope is in You.

17

Do I Appreciate Sustaining Grace?

"He fed you in the wilderness with manna, which your
ancestors had not known, in order to humble and test
you, so that in the end he might cause you to prosper."
DEUTERONOMY 8:16

I remember years of discouragement, questioning why God hadn't answered my prayers. Then one day in Bible study, Florence said, "You never hear anyone in the Bible complaining about the parting of the Red Sea. Everyone loves delivering grace. But the Israelites, like us, were not satisfied with manna. We all complain about sustaining grace."

That was me. I'd been complaining about sustaining grace.

Had God answered my prayers for deliverance with the gift of sustenance? Did I not see that God's strength and provision were an answer, too? Why was I not grateful for manna, the everyday grace of God? In waiting for monumental deliverance—the kind where I could put my issue to bed and never have to pray about it again—I'd overlooked the grace that kept drawing me to Him.

The children of Israel were familiar with the gift of dependence. They were given manna as they wandered in the wilderness, but they needed God to provide it daily. Manna taught them to rely on God and live by His word, but like me, they often scorned it. It was unexciting and monotonous, not extraordinary or glorious like the parting of the Red Sea. Manna simply provided for their needs.

I know how they felt. I don't value sustaining grace. I often overlook the way God sustains me through the day with His unfailing love. How He gives me strength when I'm weak. How He comforts me with His presence.

I want miraculous deliverance. I want the pain to stop, not just to be upheld in the pain. Yet being sustained and not delivered has done a far deeper work in my soul. It's kept me connected to God and not His gifts because it's taught me the beauty of dependence.

In delivering grace, we see God's glory. Everyone can see the miracle He has wrought for us, and if even just for a moment, our lives seem easier. We thank God for it, but we quickly go back to daily life. We may even forget what He's done because we don't need to keep going back to Him.

Unlike delivering grace which, once received, inadvertently moved me to greater independence from God, sustaining grace has kept me tethered to Him. God's glory is in that too, but the miracle He works is *in* us. This grace is not a one-time thing, just as manna was not a one-time event. We need it every day.

With sustaining grace, we get the grace to press on in the midst of trial. And we get more of Jesus—His comfort, His nearness, His presence.

As much as I long for deliverance, for delivering grace, I see the exquisite blessing in sustaining grace. It's not about getting what I want; it's about God giving me what I desperately need: Himself.

———————

REFLECT: How has receiving God's delivering grace tempted you toward independence? And how has God's sustaining grace—sustenance, provision, comfort—taught you the beauty of dependence?

18

Do You Realize That You Are in the Middle of Your Story?

*By faith we understand that the universe was
created by the word of God, so that what is seen
was made from things that are not visible.*

HEBREWS 11:3

Have you ever looked around at your life and assumed things will never get better? That there's no point in hoping anymore because it will only lead to disappointment? I have.

When my husband left, my daughters and I struggled to find our identity together and establish our new normal. Our once peaceful home was characterized by disrespect, disillusionment, and disobedience. I hated the way my story was unfolding. In my mind, intact families had kids who were drawn to God. They laughed together and talked around the dinner table. They whispered heartfelt prayers at night and respected their parents' authority. Our family didn't do those things anymore.

I couldn't see past the pain. But almost a decade later, I watched Katie be commissioned to go to Africa as a missionary. The pastor said in his sermon, "Don't be so focused on what God has taken from you that you can't see or believe that God will do something through you. . . . As Paul E. Miller says, "When confronted with suffering that won't go away or with even a minor problem, we instinctively focus on what's missing . . . not on the Master's hand. Often when you think everything has gone wrong, it's just that you're in the middle of a story."[11]

When we're in the middle of our story, it's easy to focus on what's missing and not on God's work. At one point, neither Katie nor Kristi wanted anything to do with God, even though we once prayed together every night. They both felt God had let them down and they couldn't trust Him again. They wondered why He hadn't answered their prayers. So did I.

Yet even when I couldn't see anything, God was working. Eventually, both girls came to faith, learning to depend on God for themselves. Those desperate years when God was silent, He was not absent. He'd been drawing them to Himself all along, teaching them to trust, when I was only focused on the visible.

You are in the middle of your story. You don't know how things will turn out, but you do know that nothing is impossible with God who created the universe from nothing, who gives life to the dead and calls into existence the things that do not exist.

At the same time, all our stories may not get tied up with a bow in this life. We may not see our children turn to Christ, our marriages restored, or our diseases cured. But you can trust that God is in the story. And He is the author, orchestrating the tiniest details for your final good. We can be confident that after the last chapter is written, your story will be tied up with a bow in the most glorious way possible.

WRITE: Notice the threads in your story that are unresolved. Write a letter to God, confessing the places where you cannot yet see resolution, and commit those areas to Him. Keep this letter and return to it periodically, continuing to pray or praise as your story unfolds.

Ask God for Whatever You Need

Cast all your anxiety on him because he cares for you.
1 PETER 5:7 NIV

I know I can ask God for whatever I need. But too often I think that means I shouldn't ask God for the smaller things I want. It seems more holy to contentedly trust God, especially since I don't know what's best for me. Yet when I stop telling God everything, limiting my requests solely to life-altering concerns, I have a different relationship with Him. One that seems more businesslike than like a child to her father. What draws me close to God is telling Him everything, from what I am anxious about to what delights me, and asking Him to fulfill those desires.

The fact that Jesus's first miracle was at the wedding at Cana underscores that truth. Running out of wine wasn't a life-or-death problem, but it would have led to deep embarrassment in that culture. The shortage may have been caused by human failure, but Jesus chose to fix it quietly and abundantly.

In reading about that miracle, I saw that Jesus cares about all our desires. Every need is an opportunity to trust Jesus. To see His glory. To believe in Him. If you had everything you wanted, you wouldn't be able to see how He provides. As Samuel Rutherford said, "Wants are my best riches, for I have these supplied by Christ."[12]

Recently, I noticed David asked God specifically for joy when he said, "Bring joy to your servant's life, because I appeal to you, Lord" (Ps. 86:4). David's bold request for joy surprised me. I think we all want joy, but I wonder how many of us have asked God for it.

Sometimes we find joy as we see His work demonstrated in supernatural ways, but other times it comes as we see His work as part of our daily lives. Ordinary events we could easily overlook if we weren't specifically looking for them.

Perhaps God will do the miraculous as a sign of His goodness. Or perhaps He will just open our eyes to His goodness around us.

As Mother Frances Dominica said, "We think of God in the dramatic things, the glorious sunsets, the majestic mountains, the tempestuous seas; but he is in the little things too, in the smile of a passerby, or the gnarled hands of an old man. . . . God is in the music, and laughter, and in sorrow too. And the grey times, when the monotony stretches out ahead, these can be times of steady, solid growth. . . . There is no limit to the ways in which God may make himself known."[13]

But when we are willing to ask God for both the miraculous and the mundane, bringing all our cares to Him, we can see His provision.

Jesus's first miracle was about need and joy. Some might have seen it as frivolous, but the Lord didn't think so. Knowing His delight in our joy makes me even more eager to bring everything to God, confident it won't be trivial to Him.

REFLECT: What is something mundane you want but have hesitated asking from God? And what is something miraculous you want God to do?

The Power of the Word

This I know: God is for me.

PSALM 56:9

S ome days I wake up crying.

When I do, I often don't even know why. Perhaps it's the weight of unspoken problems I'm too afraid to articulate, coupled with a vague dread of what might come next. Or perhaps it's the growing realization that the pain I'm feeling will only intensify throughout the day.

I had one of those days a while ago. As I lay in bed, contemplating what the day might hold, I felt tears welling up inside me.

"Stop, don't do this," I told myself. But I couldn't force the tears to stop, and they started trickling down my face. Before long, my pillow was soaked, and I felt hopeless.

Your life is miserable. You're a burden. You can't do anything for yourself, were the ugly voices I heard until I forced myself out of bed.

I pulled my robe on slowly and stumbled into my prayer closet. I didn't want to go, but I knew I needed this. "Please, God, help me. Show me Your truth," was my only cry. I couldn't muster anything more.

I turned to the first reading for the day, wondering what God had for me. It was Psalm 56, a beloved passage.

I knew I needed this as I read the first words, "Be gracious to me, God" (v. 1).

Then I read: "When I am afraid, I will trust in you. In God, whose word I praise, in God I trust; I will not be afraid" (vv. 3–4). I wondered if I trusted Him. Trusting felt harder today. Yet I declared those words even in my doubt. God knew I was afraid. He didn't condemn me but called me to trust Him in my pain. He alone could drive out my fears.

"You yourself have recorded my wanderings. Put my tears in your bottle. Are they not in your book?" (v. 8). God had recorded everything. All the tears I'd cried. All my fears, spoken and unspoken. It was all laid bare before Him.

Then these words took my breath away: "This I know: God is for me" (v. 9).

God is for me. Even when life looks like it's splintering, God is for me. And if God is for me, He is orchestrating every detail of my life for my good. I can trust Him even when it looks dark. He tells me not to fear because He will take care of me.

God is for me. My eyes teared up for the second time that morning, but these were tears of joy and hope. This word was truer than my circumstances. This word would sustain me. This word could revive and comfort me, with the lasting comfort of God.

As I left my prayer closet, I was grateful for the way the Lord had met me. Meeting with Him through His living Word had reframed everything.

MEMORIZE: Write today's verse on an index card. Put it where you'll see it regularly so you can memorize it.

Rock-Solid Comfort in Any Affliction

He comforts us in all our affliction, so that we may be able to comfort those who are in any kind of affliction, through the comfort we ourselves receive from God.

2 CORINTHIANS 1:4

My friend's husband had just received a cancer diagnosis. She talked to a neighbor, who first sympathized but then quickly assured her that everything would be fine.

That kind of mindless positivity felt hollow. I wonder why reassurance that the worst won't happen is our go-to comfort. Perhaps it's because we want our friends to feel better immediately. And perhaps it's because we subtly believe that God will be more glorified in healing and wholeness than in sickness and brokenness.

Is it helpful to hear anecdotes of people who had a good outcome? When I was first diagnosed with post-polio syndrome, friends felt sure I would beat the odds, which would glorify God.

But now I realize I can glorify God even though my body isn't healed. When my husband left, everyone had God-glorifying stories of broken marriages being restored. But I have learned that God can be glorified even after a heartbreaking divorce.

My friend felt her pain was being dismissed as people tried to cheer her up. She wanted true comfort. Comfort that would hold her up whether the outcome was positive or negative. Comfort that would not constantly change if the news unfolded unfavorably. Comfort that was not based on wishful thinking or the medical odds.

She had found true comfort in the Heidelberg Catechism, memorized years earlier.[14] She began with the question: "What is your only comfort in life and in death?"

She paused and then said, "That I am not my own, but belong with body and soul, both in life and in death, to my faithful Savior Jesus Christ." I was startled by the power of this simple statement. The greatest comfort we can have is knowing we belong to Jesus. That nothing can separate us from His love or snatch us from His hand.

She went on, "He has fully paid for all my sins with his precious blood and has set me free from all the power of the devil." His precious blood has redeemed me. There is no outstanding debt with God. And Satan has no power over me, so there is nothing to fear. She continued, "He also preserves me in such a way that without the will of my heavenly father not a hair can fall from my head; indeed, all things must work together for my salvation." Everything that happens to me has passed through God's hands, and He will use it all for good.

She finished, "Therefore, by his Holy Spirit, he also assures me of eternal life and makes me heartily willing and ready from now on to live for him." We can endure anything in this life on earth when we know our end is glorious.

When life falls apart, I too want to remember these precious words—timeless truths based on the eternal promises of God in Scripture. This is true comfort, and it is unchanging.

PRACTICE: Spend time memorizing the first question and answer of the Heidelberg Catechism (in quotes).[15] Repeat this daily to remember what is eternally true.

Have You Been Disappointed with God?

My days have slipped by; my plans have been ruined, even the things dear to my heart.

JOB 17:11

A friend walked away from faith a few years ago asking, "What good does God do for us anyway?"

This may sound like a startling question. But if your losses have stacked up and your dreams haven't come true or your prayers seem unanswered and God seems far away, you may be wondering the same thing.

My friend said, "You go to church, read the Bible, believe in Jesus, and try to live by godly principles. But when life comes crashing down and you sincerely cry out for help, God is strangely silent. So you begin to wonder if He ever was real in the first place. The Bible sounds like nonsense, and Christianity looks like a hoax that in the end delivers nothing but empty promises."

Have you ever felt that way? Are you tired of hoping and waiting because you're not sure what you're hoping and waiting for anyway? Maybe it's easier not to believe and just to play the cards you were dealt without waiting for a miracle. That way you won't be disappointed.

If those words resonate with you, I understand, at least partially, how you feel. I have not walked away from my faith, but I have felt let down by God. I wondered where He was as I felt my prayers weren't even being heard. My main goal was changed circumstances, so my prayer list was made up of the things I wanted God to change.

When it didn't happen, I questioned God. I echoed Larry Crabb's words when he wrote, "I couldn't shake the assumption that the display of God's glory meant the enjoyment of my story. If he loves me, he will bless me. What I did not see was that he wanted to bless me with himself. I was too much like the spoiled child at Christmas who really didn't much care if dad showed up on Christmas morning as long as he had stacked lots of presents beneath the tree."[16]

I assumed that if God loved me, He would bless me. It took me a while to see that I could trust God to use the exact hand He dealt me to maximize my joy. Nothing was accidental. And I saw that the greatest gift was not a comfortable life but clinging to Him in a life that was far from comfortable.

I still pray for my friend. I want her to see the absolute beauty and goodness of God, to understand that this life will be over in the twinkling of an eye, and to believe God has eternity to show us the immeasurable riches of His grace.

PRAY: Lord, I confess that I have doubted You when things haven't gone my way. When You've felt distant. When my prayers to You seem to be unanswered. Please forgive me and open my eyes to Your absolute love, beauty, and goodness today.

23

Can We Control God through Our Obedience?

Protect me, God, for I take refuge in you.
I said to the LORD, "You are my Lord;
I have nothing good besides you."
PSALM 16:1–2

I was having coffee with a couple I'd recently met, as we each shared our lives and our stories. I'd just told them about Paul's death, which was on the heels of three miscarriages. Before I could finish, the husband interrupted me and said, "Don't take this wrong, but we prayed for our children, and all of them were born healthy."

I sat in silence for a few seconds as I took in his words. How exactly did he expect me to take that remark?

Did he think I hadn't prayed? Were they blaming me for our son's death? Did he believe my miscarriages were all my fault?

My mind was reeling after that conversation, but this attitude wasn't new. From the day we learned of Paul's heart problem when I was pregnant, concerned friends assured me Paul would be fine if we prayed in faith. So I did. But months later, sitting beside Paul's empty crib, I had more questions than answers. What had I done wrong? Why didn't God heal Paul?

After a long time of searching, I realized that I'd always assumed my faithfulness would result in God's blessings. That trouble was a result of my failings. And that by fulfilling my end of the relationship, God would have to fulfill His.

Tim Keller referred to this subtle but dangerous expectation when he wrote, "If, like the elder brother, you seek to control God through your obedience, then all your morality is just a way to use God to make him give you the things in life you really want."[17]

That was exactly how I viewed things.

As I searched the Bible for answers, I realized that my delight needed to be in God and not His gifts. The best gift He can give me is not health or healing or happiness *but more of Himself.* And that gift is often clearest in suffering. Even when everything in life fails, I can cling to God, who is my portion forever.

I don't know what's best for me. I want easy answers, fill-in-the-blanks, pain-free predictability. I want a paint-by-numbers life. But God is not after comfortable mediocrity. His artistry is unrivaled. He is creating masterpieces. God brushes unexpected color across the canvas of our lives, says no when we beg for yes, and offers His presence when we want His presents—because He has a much bigger plan for us. A plan that glorifies Him and brings us everlasting delight.

I realized that others, like this couple, might not understand the gifts God gave me when my prayers weren't answered exactly as I'd asked. To them, the outcome reflected my lack of faith or weak prayers. Yet I know God always hears us and wants to give us His very best, sparing nothing that would be good for us. God is always there, faithfully walking with us through every trial. And His presence is a far greater gift than any outcome we can imagine.

REFLECT: How have you been tempted to believe that your faithfulness would result in God's blessings? And what would it look like to release a "God owes me" ideology, knowing that the true riches of God are found in His presence?

24

A Format for Lament

During his earthly life, he offered prayers and
appeals with loud cries and tears to the one
who was able to save him from death, and
he was heard because of his reverence.

HEBREWS 5:7

Lamenting feels uncomfortable for me because I'm not sure if we can be honest with God about how upset we really are. I imagine that more holy Christians trust God with everything, offering endless words of thanks and praise. They always rejoice in the Lord, without a hint of discouragement or complaint. Nothing gets them down. Or at least that's what I've always told myself.

Yet I'm learning God wants the authentic *me*, not the *me* that uses church words to cover my pain. God knows my heart and what honors Him most are honest words. The psalmists were shockingly candid with God, and through their wrestling, they modeled how to worship God with tears. Scripture never mandates that we constantly be upbeat. God wants us to come to Him in truth. And so the Bible doesn't whitewash the raw emotions of its writers who cry out to God in anguish, fear, and frustration when life doesn't make sense.

Lament may sound like grumbling, but the spirit behind it is different. Grumblers want to talk *about* God, not *to* Him. Their questions are accusations, and their mind is made up as they bitterly withdraw. Those who wrestle want to understand, they want God to draw near, they want God's presence in their pain. They are trusting and searching, looking to God. Lamenters work out their problems with God *with* God. As Clint Watkins says, "You may feel that God is being unloving or unmerciful. But instead of turning those feelings into a conclusion, lament helps you turn them into a conversation."[18]

Coming to God with loud cries and tears honors God. That's how Jesus prayed, and it was described as reverence. Following Jesus's example, you too can cry out and ask God to remove the bitter cup before you.

In most laments, the writers tell God how they're feeling about their situation, ask for what they want, and finally express words of trust. These elements can be in any order, but this is the most natural flow for me.

The truths we voice after lament are God infused. We learn to trust God even when we cannot understand our sorrows. When I write my lament, as the psalmists and Jeremiah (the author of Lamentations) did, I sense His movement in my life. He comforts me. He fills me with hope. He bears my sorrows.

WRITE: You may want to work on this over a few days, doing one prompt per day. For each one, try to write two to three sentences.[19]

1. Spend some time thinking through areas of past pain in your life, and then pick one to focus on.
2. Describe the situation and the destruction it caused.
3. Pour out your painful feelings, whatever they are, to God. Don't hold back.
4. Cry out to God for help, boldly asking for whatever you want Him to do.
5. Remember what you know to be true about God and His faithfulness to you.

25

Even in the Darkest Valley

Even when I go through the darkest valley,
I fear no danger, for you are with me.
PSALM 23:4

I'm amazed at how the Lord uses our words to encourage others and how they in turn come back to encourage us. That's how I felt when I received this letter about an article I'd written ten years earlier:

> I want to tell you how much your article "What If the Worst Happens" has meant to me. I have an adult son who wanted to alligator hunt for the meat. His daddy died when he was quite young and I filled in for many of the roles dads do, so it was natural that he asked me to go gator hunting with him. But boy I was scared. Originally, the state of Florida only allowed us to hunt at night. You flash flashlights around the water until you spot two glowing eyes, and then the hunt begins.

Hunting season here is always during our rainy season and I was petrified.

Sometimes horrifying lightning struck all around our tiny boat as we tried to find shore from the blinding rain, trying not to drown. Our tent, clothing, boat, and belongings were always drenched. I never prayed so much and so hard, which is a lot to say since I am in my late 70s. I prayed nonstop while we hunted and during the week. I even dreamt prayers. Then I read your article and it was revolutionary to me. I asked myself, "What if the boat capsizes? What if we fall into the water with the gators? What if one of us dies while hunting?" I realized that even if the worst happened, dead or alive, our lives would go on because we have Jesus.

Everything changed after "what if" became ingrained in my heart. I made signs reading "WHAT IF" and posted them everywhere—on the TV, computer, mirrors, boat, tackle, everywhere. "What if" became my mantra and I firmly believed we could handle anything and all the "what ifs" that could happen on our hunting trips. It has changed me and how I am living this life on earth. I have let go of all fear and totally trust Jesus.

Love in Christ, Mary

If Mary, in her seventies, could trust God without fear while gator hunting in a small boat in a lightning storm, how could I not trust God? Mary's "what if" was a beautiful reminder that even if the worst happens, God is with us. The day I received Mary's letter had been particularly challenging, and God used her to remind me that no matter what I was going through, even if the worst happened, He would be everything I needed.

REFLECT: What is the "gator hunt" going on in your life right now? How does Mary's "WHAT IF" make a difference in your perspective?

26

The Greatest Turn in Scripture

Yet I call this to mind,
and therefore I have hope:
Because of the LORD's faithful love
we do not perish, for his mercies never end.
They are new every morning; great is your faithfulness!
LAMENTATIONS 3:21–23

Can anything help us rise above an experience that was unforgettably hard? Perhaps experiencing something more spectacular, so remarkable it can overshadow our pain. We see that in childbirth, which can be excruciatingly painful. But when a baby is born, a mother can look past all the pain in the joy and delight of her newborn infant. But can we do that in the middle of pain, when the pain is not in the past but rather is still present?

Jeremiah shows us how. He was in anguish for both himself and his people. He felt hopeless and trampled on, certain he would never forget the awful time he'd just been through. He was certain God was against him and outlined his agony in a breathless stream of anger and discouragement (Lam. 3:1–20)

Jeremiah suddenly stopped in the middle of his complaint and looked at God. After his cascade of words, he was noticeably calmer. He began seeing through a different lens, drawing close and remembering who God is. Perhaps in trusting God with all his rage and disappointment, in holding nothing back and sharing exactly how he felt, Jeremiah could finally let go of his despair.

After Jeremiah seemed to say everything he could think of, he paused to remember God's faithfulness. Then Jeremiah uttered what is perhaps the greatest shift in all of Scripture as he said, "This I call to mind and therefore I have hope" (NIV). In the midst of torment, Jeremiah chose to remember something greater.

Nothing had changed in Jeremiah's life. But as he considered the character of God, he saw his situation differently. He remembered God's unfailing love and mercy. God's faithfulness. God's blessings that were new every morning.

Remembering and rehearsing what's true about God is a critical step to walking well in suffering. Remembering that everything in our lives flows out of the goodness and faithfulness of God. Remembering that God loves us fiercely and will never leave us. And remembering that our hope is not in changed circumstances but in the character of God. He is our living hope.

Dramatic turnarounds like Jeremiah's, when no light has dawned, when no miracles have delivered you, when you're still living amid the unthinkable, may seem impossible. If you're willing to stare straight into the abyss with God, telling Him all that you're feeling and seeing, leaning hard into Him in your pain, you will experience a cataclysmic shift in your soul. It may be sudden or gradual, but it will surely come. Your faith will take on a supernatural strength and confidence. And you will know, from experience and not just academically, how the greatest turns in our faith, our greatest revelations of God, come from our greatest pain.

MEMORIZE: Write today's verse on an index card. Put it where you'll see it regularly so you can memorize it.

27

You Are Not Missing Out

By his divine power, God has given us
everything we need for living a godly life.
2 PETER 1:3 NLT

A deep sadness would often come over me when people talked about encountering God in nature. Being outside is never restful for me. With my poor circulation, I get chilled or overheated quickly. Besides, since I can't navigate uneven terrain, I need help when I'm outside.

For years I felt I was missing out on something integral to a strong faith. When friends would rave about the inexplicable closeness they had with God in nature, I longed to experience that myself. While I know God displays His handiwork in nature, my firsthand knowledge was largely limited to what I could see through windows.

Someone once took me to a beautiful waterfall so I could experience it myself. When we got there, I found a bench and marveled at the beauty around me. I talked to God and soaked in the silence, anticipating a profound sense of His presence. I desperately wanted this to be an unforgettable experience. I waited and prayed, but it didn't feel supernatural or holy. I didn't feel close to God there. I almost felt distant because I was trying so hard to feel something.

When we left, I cried out to God, "Why? When I have so few opportunities to be outside to experience You in nature, why did You not meet me?"

When I got home, I sat by the window in my room and stared outside. It really was beautiful. I opened my Bible and read Psalm 19: "The heavens declare the glory of God, and the sky above proclaims his handiwork" (v. 1 ESV).

Why had those words felt hollow earlier? Staring at the beauty behind glass, those words were now rich with meaning. God was glorious. I saw His handiwork in nature as I noticed the tall pines swaying in the wind.

I felt God's presence as I had many times before. This was where God always meets me. This was our place, with me sitting at a table, my Bible open and journal in hand. This was where I'd learned to hear God's voice.

I wasn't missing out. I didn't need to go anywhere special to experience God. He wanted to meet me just where I was—in the ordinary, everyday spaces of my life. I didn't need to feel jealous that other people climbed mountains and sat by beautiful streams to commune with God. It wasn't the place that mattered; what mattered was the encounter with God.

Since the Lord has given us all we need for life and godliness, we lack nothing. But Satan tries to convince us that we are missing out as he hisses, "If you only had this, your life would be better." Satan told Eve that lie in the garden, and he has been whispering it to us since then. Don't believe it.

I am not missing out and neither are you. God is giving us all we need.

REFLECT: Where does the enemy tempt you to believe you're missing out? Ask God to bring to your mind the truth about His trustworthy provision in all circumstances.

Does Grief Frighten You?

Be gracious to me, O LORD,
for I am in distress;
my eye is wasted from grief;
my soul and my body also.
PSALM 31:9 ESV

I don't like to grieve for long. I want to move on, to get things accomplished, to feel like my grief has done something good for me. I want to know how long it's going to take and what I need to do to get past it.

When Paul died, grief looked like frenzied creativity at first. I painted a set of dishes, working late into the night, pouring my energy into making something beautiful. At first my busyness felt like a way to work through my pain, but after months of feverish work, I still felt empty. I couldn't move past the grief that quickly. As Tish Harrison Warren says, "We want grief to be a task we can complete. The oven timer of our soul dings and we're on to something else. But that isn't how grief works. We control it as much as we control the weather."[20]

I wanted to complete the task of grieving, but it wouldn't magically end. I knew I had to process my grief with God, but I'd emotionally disconnected from Him and His Word, finding little comfort in either. Partly because I felt God had let me down. And partly because I was afraid of where my honest thoughts would lead. Would they lead me away from God?

With hesitation, I began to lament, talking to God, not sure where it would take me. I brought to Him the unprocessed and the messy. I admitted my unspoken fears. I cried, wailed, and wrote furiously, unleashing everything that was inside. I wondered if the process would pull me from God, but instead it drew me closer.

When we lament, God invites us to explore our feelings with Him, even when we don't know what they are. For me it begins with sitting in front of a blank page, Bible open, ready to figure out with God what's going on inside me. And when I start writing, words tumble out, emotions long hidden, startling me with their intensity.

Journaling my lament has deeply connected me to God. When I write, God exposes what's in my heart. It's like counseling, where we better understand ourselves as we uncover the lies we've long believed. Yet here we are processing with the wisest counselor, who knows and sees everything.

Despite how life-changing lament has been for me, I'm still often hesitant to start. It feels messy and unpredictable and doesn't tie up into a neat theological bow. I write things I'd never hear in church. So if it feels a bit scary to you, you're not alone. But trust God with the process, that He will go with you even into the darkest places and bring you back into the light.

———————

PRAY: Lord, I'm afraid to even admit to myself, let alone You, what I'm feeling. Help me to be real with You, and please guide my words and thoughts, bringing out the deep things in my heart that only You know. I trust You with the process, confident that You are with me in the darkest places.

29

Being Rescued from Fear

I sought the LORD, and he answered me
and rescued me from all my fears.
PSALM 34:4

I need the Lord to rescue me from fear. Not just to rescue me from the things that I'm afraid of but also to rescue me from being afraid. The Message translates Psalm 34:4 this way: "GOD met me more than halfway, he freed me from my anxious fears." How does God free us from our fears? It happens when we seek God, ask Him for help, and put our trust in Him.

When my ex-husband left, the night held terrors for my daughters and me. Katie, the eldest at thirteen, was afraid we were vulnerable and unprotected and had planned an escape route to rescue me and Kristi if necessary. I was afraid of a fire, wondering how I'd get my daughters out or what I'd do if someone broke in. And Kristi was afraid of dangers across multiple categories, mentally cataloging all that could go wrong.

None of our fears were realized, but our past record didn't keep us from being afraid. What helped us was reciting Psalm 34, trusting that the angel of the Lord was encamping around us and would rescue us when we cried out to Him (vv. 7, 15).

Looking back over my life, I see that I've been concerned about so many problems that never came to pass. Some of my fears did materialize, and like Job, I could say, "The thing I feared has overtaken me, and what I dreaded has happened to me" (Job 3:25). Yet even in those nightmares, I discovered that fear and dread didn't do any good. Pre-grieving and feeling prepared for the worst didn't make the situation any easier. Worry cannot add to our lives; it only subtracts.

Leviticus talks about the curse of fear, that people would be so filled with anxiety that they'd flee at the sound of a leaf though no one was pursuing them (Lev. 26:36). Being afraid when there's nothing to fear is an anxiety that cannot be contained or reasoned with. Irrational fears do not simply disappear because someone tells us they are not real.

Fear is often an instinctive reaction, not based on fact. And anxiety is a false prophet, making predictions that won't come true, robbing today of its peace. As Alexander McLaren said, "And what does your anxiety do? It does not empty to-morrow, brother, of its sorrows; but, ah! it empties to-day of its strength."[21]

Fear robs us of joy and strength. Since we cannot know tomorrow, we must trust God with it. When we are afraid, the surest path to peace is to put our trust in God as David did when he said, "When I am afraid, I will trust in you" (Ps. 56:3). And when we do, that act alone will dispel our fears, and we can also echo with David, "In God I trust; I will not be afraid" (Ps. 56:4).

———————

REFLECT: What anxieties rob you of joy and strength? And what is one practical way you can release your anxiety to God?

30

The Ache of Unfulfilled Longings

Lord, my every desire is in front of you;
my sighing is not hidden from you.
PSALM 38:9

I longed to remarry after my divorce but didn't want to admit it to anyone. I didn't want to pin my hopes on something that might never happen. So I buried my feelings.

At times those stuffed feelings would resurface, and I would ask God for a husband, journal about it, and pray fervently. Then I would try to forget about my longings, surrender them to God, and convince myself I didn't want to be married anyway. I told myself, and other people, that it wasn't important, that I was completely content, that I had come to terms with where I was. It seemed that everyone who loved God was satisfied with their circumstances. Besides, it seemed better to deny a longing that might never be fulfilled than it was to keep longing. It certainly was less painful.

I did remarry, which was an incredible grace, but other longings have felt just as intense, and they haven't been fulfilled. Longings for a healthy body, with arms that work and can care for myself, a body that doesn't get weaker every day. I long to watercolor paint, to entertain friends, to make gourmet meals, and even to just straighten up the counter myself. When those longings well up, I don't want to deny my pain and pretend everything is fine when it isn't. God knows my desires and wants me to go to Him with them.

We all have longings. Crying out to God to fulfill them, or change them, or give us the strength to endure them strengthens our faith. Denying our longings under the pretense of contentment may keep us from pain, look more spiritual, and make us less emotional, but can lead to spiritual deadness.

God may miraculously deliver you, and if He does, you can rejoice and thank Him. He makes all things new and brings beauty from ashes. Sometimes you won't be delivered, but He can change your desires and give you lasting contentment even when He denies your cherished requests. That can be a great gift as well. You can still rejoice by returning to the true and everlasting source of your joy.

Yet sometimes you may continue to feel those raw places in your soul, and the longing may not diminish. It might even grow stronger every year. Then you may feel His embrace most tightly as He strengthens your heart. This relentless ache has driven me to my knees, brought me to Jesus, and made me long for heaven. And perhaps in heaven, we will all thank God most for our unfulfilled longings because they did the deepest, most lasting work in our souls.

———————

WRITE: Ask God to show you what unfulfilled longing He wants you to offer Him today. Write a letter to God, describing what is hard about that longing, not minimizing or dismissing the pain. What have you lost? Pour out your heart to Him, knowing that He loves you more than you can know.

31

Why It's Better
to Have a Trouble

You provided for them in the wilderness
forty years, and they lacked nothing.
NEHEMIAH 9:21

My friends once prayed that I'd be like the widow of Zarephath, that I'd have enough strength and energy for each day. And the supply, while I couldn't see it, would never run out.

While I love this story in 1 Kings 17, I don't want to be like this widow. Elijah said she'd have just enough oil and flour for each day. She had no resources of her own, but she had God, who provided for her daily.

Her story is a beautiful picture of dependence on God. Beautiful, that is, for others. Personally, I don't like being dependent.

But in the last few decades, my life has been characterized by dependence—on friends, family, and God. With post-polio syndrome, I must trust God to supply the strength I need each day. The doctors say my strength is like money in a bank. I can make withdrawals but no deposits. When it runs out, there is no more. Since I have no idea how much reserve is left, I must trust God to give me the energy I need each day.

As a result, friends have prayed that God would provide for me as He did the widow. What a reassuring picture for my future. Utter dependence on God. Seeing Him provide for my needs. Trusting Him when I cannot see.

Yet that picture doesn't feel reassuring to me. I want a full oil flask and an overflowing flour bin. I'd rather depend on myself than on God, with God as my backup plan, but I know God has something better in mind. For all of us.

That doesn't mean we don't plan or want God's material blessings. But our desire for security and circumstantial satisfaction could be keeping us from a deeper walk with God. It's wonderful to have great health and never go to the doctor. But being ill may cause us to pray more earnestly.

Charles Spurgeon said, "There is no greater mercy that I know of on earth than good health except it be sickness; and that has often been a greater mercy to me than health. It is a good thing to be without a trouble; but it is a better thing to have a trouble and know how to get grace enough to bear it."[22]

Anything that makes us dependent on God is a good thing, perhaps the best thing. Our fellowship with God is the sweetest when we rely on Him for everything. Through the wilderness the children of Israel learned to depend on God.

Our places of desolation can become the places where we see God the most clearly. Not only does He meet our every need, but He wondrously fills us with Himself.

———————

REFLECT: Where have you witnessed this upside-down economy of God's grace, finding mercy in sickness or trouble? And what is the place of desolation *today* in which you need to depend on God?

When We Are Worried about the Future

The Lord is near. Don't worry about anything, but in everything, through prayer and petition with thanksgiving, present your requests to God. And the peace of God, which surpasses all understanding, will guard your hearts and minds in Christ Jesus.

PHILIPPIANS 4:5–7

How will this turn out? How hard will it be? How long is this trial going to last? Those questions are often at the core of my worries. I want reassurance that my worries are unfounded and that everything will turn out well.

Some time ago, I was concerned about an unexplained new health issue, uncertain of what the underlying problem might be. I was sitting before an open Bible, but my mind was far away.

I grabbed my phone and put my questions into Google. I wanted to understand what I might be dealing with, so I kept scrolling to look up more information. After finding a few hopeful answers, I still felt unsettled. My worries were eroding my peace. I went back to reading my Bible, wishing I hadn't interrupted my time with the Lord for the allure of Google-driven confidence.

Then I read, "God is our refuge and strength, a helper who is always found in times of trouble. Therefore we will not be afraid, though the earth trembles" (Ps. 46:1–2). Immediately I was convicted. Why did I think that my problem was a lack of information? Why did I want reassurance from the world rather than from God? Why hadn't I brought my worries to Him?

I sat there praying, confessing my lack of trust, and telling God everything I wanted. I poured out my questions, my desires, and my fears, and then I felt my heart settle. I knew God was with me and would be with me no matter the outcome.

Peace doesn't come from information or understanding; it comes from the presence of God. The Lord is near. Because the Lord is always near, we can have a peace that surpasses understanding.

I instinctively wrote, "God knows all about the boats."

Elisabeth Elliot introduced me to that phrase when she wrote of Amy Carmichael's experience as a young missionary in Japan. Amy and an older couple were delayed by a boat that never came, and they had to wait days for the next boat to arrive. Amy worried about the lost time and inconvenience to others, to which the older missionary calmly responded, "God knows all about the boats."[23]

"God knows all about the boats" became a lifelong maxim to Amy, and now to me, reminding me that God is in control and knows every detail of what is happening. Even when I'm waiting for answers, I don't need to worry.

So the next time I'm worried about something, instead of turning to the world for reassurance, I pray that I will not fear what is happening, will not turn to Google over God, and will rest knowing that even if the worst happens, God will always be by my side.

———————

MEMORIZE: Write today's verse on an index card. Put it where you'll see it regularly so you can memorize it.

33

The Loneliness of Suffering

Rest in God alone, my soul, for
my hope comes from him.
PSALM 62:5

One of the hardest things for me about suffering is loneliness. When loss is fresh, people are all around. They call, offer help, send cards, and bring meals. Their care helps ease the razor-sharp pain. For a while.

But then they stop. There are no more meals. The phone is strangely silent. And the mailbox is empty. No one knows what to say. They aren't sure what to ask. So mostly they say nothing.

Sometimes that's fine. It's hard to talk about pain. And I never want pity, with the mournful look, the squeeze on the arm, and the hushed question, "So, how are you?" I don't know how to answer that; I don't know how I am. Part of me is crushed; I will never be the same again.

On good days, we appreciate our friends' efforts and recognize they're busy, but on bad days, we wonder why people aren't meeting our needs, especially the emotional ones. At least, that's what I do. I forget there's a part of suffering I must bear myself.

In Galatians 6:2 (ESV), Paul says, "Bear one another's burdens, and so fulfill the law of Christ." And then he says, "For each will have to bear his own load" (v. 5 ESV).

The word Paul uses for "burden" implies burdens that exceed our strength. In Paul's day, travelers often had to transport heavy loads that others would carry for a while to ease the burden. This could be likened to our service, prayers, physical presence.

His word for "load" is proportioned to our individual strength. That could be the ongoing work of processing our grief. The parts of suffering no one else can carry for us.

Even the most caring friends cannot be with us in our deepest pain. They may weep with us, but they cannot always walk with us. In Jesus's moments of greatest need, His friends deserted Him, and He found himself alone with God. Just as we often are.

So, what do we do when no one understands our suffering and we feel unbearably lonely?

Read the Bible and pray. Read the Bible even when it feels like eating cardboard. And pray even when it feels like talking to a wall.

Does it sound simple? It is. Does it also sound exceedingly hard? It is that as well. But reading the Bible and praying are the only way I have ever found out of my grief.

As much as I've wanted my friends to comfort me, no one has ever met me the way God has. No one's words have ever changed me the way Scripture has. And no one's presence has ever encouraged me the way the Holy Spirit has.

My friends have helped, but they've never healed me. Only God can do that. And this path of suffering, of heartache, of loneliness takes me directly to my Savior, which is the lone path worth taking. For only Jesus can heal me.

———————

REFLECT: What burden is heaviest on your heart today? Would you actively release it to God right now?

34

How to Live When You Know You're Dying

For me, to live is Christ and to die is gain.
PHILIPPIANS 1:21

My husband Joel's first wife, Barb, taught him how to trust God as she bravely fought cancer. Near the end of her life, their pastor commented, "We have all been praying for healing for Barb and asking for a miracle. But perhaps the greater miracle is not healing but watching someone trust God and live faithfully even when they are facing death."

Living faithfully while facing death. I want to do that.

Years ago, I received an email from Patrick, whose wife Becky had died of cancer. He sent me an excerpt from a letter she had written to a friend:

Dear Sister in Christ,

A mutual friend recently asked me to correspond with you. She knows I'm a cancer survivor and thought I might have some words of encouragement to offer. The timing of her letter was utterly ironic; I'd just been told that my cancer has spread to both lungs. I'm in the trenches with you so these words don't come from distant memories but from present realities.

1. Recognizing that most of our battles are waged in the mind, I choose to focus on God. Nothing can come into my life that is not first filtered through the fingers of God's love. God knew before the foundation of the world that I'd have cancer and has already provided the resources I need to face it.

2. I chose to view this illness as a gift. It is a time to draw near to God, to experience God more fully, to enjoy the simple joys of life, to focus on those things that are truly important.

3. Although cancer wants to be an all-encompassing issue in my life, I refuse to sink within myself. I will reach out to someone else each day with a letter, word of encouragement, act of service, or prayer.

4. I will not ignore my emotions. I will allow myself to cry as necessary in order to vent my feelings, but I will NOT be ruled by them.

5. I will share what is happening with others and enlist their support and prayers.

6. I will make both short-term and long-term goals in order to have something to look forward to. I will endeavor to keep my life as "normal" as possible as long as I am physically able so I won't slide into introspection and self-pity.

7. I will find some reason to laugh every day.

8. I will remind myself that, in some inexplicable way, the way I conduct myself during this time of struggle does impact the spiritual world.

I love this letter because it's practical, honest, and God centered. I'm praying that one day, like Becky and Barb, I will live faithfully when facing death.

———————

PRAY: Lord, no matter what my circumstances, help me to keep my eyes on You, receiving what You have set before me. Help me appreciate the small joys You bring every day and remember that the way I conduct myself matters even if I don't know how.

Do You Wonder
If God Cares?

"If the LORD is with us, why then
has all this happened to us?"
JUDGES 6:13 ESV

I f the Lord is with us, why then has all this happened to us?"
Gideon asked the question thousands of years ago, and we
have been asking it ever since.

The Israelites were disheartened by the Midianites' continual
oppression. These hardships didn't make sense if God was with
His people. They had heard stories of God's power, but since they
hadn't seen it displayed, they wondered if He was with them at
all.

That's why Gideon asked the angel of the Lord, almost
desperately, "Where are all his wonderful deeds that our fathers
recounted to us?" He followed his question with bleak despair:
"But now the LORD has forsaken us" (Judg. 6:13 ESV).

Looking at the circumstances, Gideon saw no evidence that God was there or that God cared.

For years I felt like Gideon. I wondered why hard things happened when God was supposedly in control.

As a child, I lived in and out of the hospital. Throughout my childhood and adolescence, I was convinced that a good God couldn't love me and watch me suffer. When people told me God loved me, I thought, *If God loves me, then why did this happen to me?* I was sure that God wasn't good, didn't exist, or didn't care. But when I came to Christ, my perspective on suffering changed. I realized God was using my disability for His glory.

I had long known the truth, but when Paul died, I returned to the familiar question: *If God loves me, then why did this happen?*

Even as I was questioning God's love, He drew near to me and showed me that His presence and love are guaranteed to those in Christ. When Satan tempts me to question God, I'm learning to stand on the truth of Scripture. In love, God sent His own Son to die for our sins. Nothing can separate me from His love.

The familiar childhood song echoes that truth: "Jesus loves me, this I know. For the Bible tells me so."

Since His love is a rock-solid guarantee, we must reframe our question and ask instead: "*Because* God loves me, why did this happen?"

Because God loves me. When I'm confident that everything in my life is a result of God's love, I can view my situation through a new lens. While I still may not know why "this" happened, I can trust that there is a "why."

If the Lord is bringing trials into your life, trust that He's doing something incredible in you, for you, and through you. *Because* the Lord is with you, and *because* the Lord loves you, everything that happens to you is filled with divine purpose. It has all passed through God's loving hands, and one day, when your faith becomes sight, you will see His love in all you've endured.

REFLECT: Have you ever asked, "If God loves me, why did this happen?" Think back to that time. Rephrase the question to ask, "Because God loves me, why did this happen?" Does this reframe your thinking? How? What changed?

36

How to Pray When Life Falls Apart

"Abba, Father, all things are possible for
you. Remove this cup from me. Yet not
what I will, but what you will."
MARK 14:36 ESV

In the midst of broken dreams and relentless pain, how should we pray?

Should we pray for healing and deliverance, believing we just need to ask, because God can do anything? Or should we relinquish our desires to God, trusting that even in our anguish He has the perfect plan for us?

Yes. When life falls apart, God invites us to do both.

Right now, I'm wondering if I'll ever walk again for more than two minutes at a time. It's been that way for a year, and no signs point to that changing. I vacillate between begging and trusting. Jesus's example helps me know how to pray.

In the garden of Gethsemane, Jesus was facing unimaginable suffering when He prayed, "Abba, Father, all things are possible for you. Remove this cup from me. Yet not what I will, but what you will" (Mark 14:36 ESV).

Jesus, in His agony, modeled how to pray when life falls apart. He began with "Abba," an intimate, personal term for a father. Jesus was asking His Father to do something for Him, and I too need to approach Him as my Father. To know that I'm His beloved, and He will not withhold anything good from me.

Jesus knew God can do absolutely anything. Nothing is impossible for God, so I don't need to limit my prayers to what doctors deem possible. God can change my situation with a word.

Even if I think God can use my suffering for His glory, it's okay to beg Him to remove the suffering before me. Jesus knew He had come to face the cross, yet in His anguish He asked God to take it away. So many times I filter my requests. Should I ask God to relieve my suffering when I know He can use it? Should I be content with what God's given me? Yet because Jesus boldly asked if there was any other way, I know I can too.

Ultimately, Jesus relinquished His will to the Father, accepting the decision without murmur or complaint. This step is hard for me since I hold tightly to the outcome I want. I may verbalize, "Your will be done," but I often just want my will. I need to remember that God is working for my good and that He has a purpose in His denials.

The Father said no to the Son, which brought about the greatest good in all of history.

For now, I must trust that God's refusals are always His mercies. And even as I struggle to make sense of my pain, I can follow Jesus's example in prayer—drawing near to God, believing He can change my situation, boldly asking Him for what I need and submitting my will to his.

WRITE: Spend time with God by writing out and exploring each phrase of Jesus's prayer in Mark 14:36.

1. "Abba, Father" (Talk to God using the names you know Him by.)
2. "All things are possible for you." (Renew your trust in His limitless power.)
3. "Remove this cup from me." (Ask for what you want.)
4. "Yet not what I will, but what you will." (Release your desires, submitting to God's will.)

Knowing the End

*"For I will create new heavens and a new earth; the
past events will not be remembered or come to mind."*
ISAIAH 65:17

My mom likes everything to be happy. Before she starts reading a novel, she turns to the last page to make sure it ends well. We tease her that she's obsessed with happy endings, but we all know that the end is critical—it gives the story meaning. That's true for our lives as well. Knowing the end can give us comfort as we live the story.

Cameron Cole says, "What if the afterlife were some amorphous, undefined mystery? If you have no end, you have no story. If you have no story, you have no ultimate sense of stability and comfort in life. Have you ever watched a dramatic, suspenseful movie for the first time, not knowing how the story would end? The experience produces anxiety and inner turmoil. However, if you go back and watch the film a second or third time . . . the conflicts and twists in the plot become less unsettling because you know the final resolution."[24]

Knowing the end makes the entire process less tumultuous. We can relax knowing our stories will turn out amazingly, though we may feel anxious at times as we wonder: Will my health be restored? Will I have a fulfilling marriage? Will I have children who love me? Will I be financially stable? I've asked all those questions at various points. Maybe you've asked similar ones too.

These conflicts and twists in the plots of our lives are unsettling, and we long to fast-forward through the difficult scenes to know how things will turn out. Yet however they unfold, we know the end of our story. We are headed for glory with a breathtaking ending. Everything we've lost and longed for will one day be transformed and redeemed. And that knowledge should change everything about today for us. It should put this life in a different perspective. Nothing on earth will last forever, but every glorious blessing will be unending in heaven.

Yet often we are immersed in the now, concerned about what is happening today. Heaven seems too far away to care about, so our energies are poured into figuring out this life. Our perspective can look frighteningly like the world, as we give into fear and even hopelessness.

We live and act as if God is dead or is at least not faithful; we don't see Christ as the perfect Redeemer; we act as if God's Word isn't true, and we doubt His complete power to hold us to the end.

If any of that were true, we might give into mourning and to despair.

What gives us everlasting hope is that God is alive, Christ has redeemed us, and all of God's promises are true. Your life will culminate in the happiest of endings, so don't judge your life by what's happening today. As Elisabeth Elliot said: "Of one thing I am perfectly sure: God's story never ends with ashes."[25]

REFLECT: Where are you questioning the plotline in your life, wondering how it will turn out? And what changes inside you when you choose to believe that God has a good ending for your story?

38

Giving Thanks When We Don't Feel Like It

Give thanks to the LORD, for he is good,
for his steadfast love endures forever!
PSALM 107:1 ESV

While this is a great verse to recite when things are going well, it's even more powerful when I repeat it when things are falling apart. It helps me remember what I know to be true, spurring me to thank God in both the good and the hard. And that thankfulness is often what God uses to turn my heart.

Giving thanks when things are falling apart is an intentional act, the opposite of my tendency to complain about difficult situations. Now I am not a proponent of the "count your blessings" cliché, forcing people to be cheerful when things are painful. Yet when I preach this verse to myself, declaring these words are true, not only do they change my attitude, but they also have the power to change my circumstances.

In 2 Chronicles 20, Jehoshaphat turned to the Lord for help when he learned his enemies were coming to attack him. He admitted his powerlessness, asked God for help, and then chose musicians to sing, "Give thanks to the LORD. . . . His steadfast love endures forever" (v. 21 ESV) as they went before the army. And immediately afterward, the Lord set an ambush, and their enemies annihilated one another in battle. The Israelites simply praised God, and He did all the rest.

Praise can drive away our enemies, which in suffering are often discouragement and desperation. I have repeated Psalm 107:1 through clenched teeth when I didn't feel I had anything to be thankful for. When what was happening in front of me didn't feel good at all and I wondered what God was doing. When I didn't feel loved and cherished but rather felt alone and abandoned. And praise has shifted the battle by driving away the lies of the enemy.

"Give thanks to the LORD. . . . His steadfast love endures forever."

Repeating these words, stopping to ponder each word, has brought me back to the truth. The truth I have built my life on, truth that reframes my suffering, truth that helps me see beyond my circumstances. Paul tells us to give thanks in all circumstances, reinforcing that giving thanks, especially when things are difficult, is good for us. Thankfulness is possible when we believe God is good and everything He does is good. We build our lives on the goodness of God. His love for us is steadfast and sure. Everything that comes into our lives flows out of that love.

His love will never fail, enduring not only through this life but eternally through the life to come.

When everything around you seems to be going wrong, I wonder if these words will ground you as well and encourage you to thank God because He is good and because you can trust His heart, even when you can't understand what is happening. This may shift something inside you. These God-breathed words of Scripture have extraordinary power to change all of us. They've changed me.

MEMORIZE: Write today's verse on an index card. Put it where you'll see it regularly so you can memorize it.

39

Redemption May Be Closer Than You Think

Put your hope in the LORD.
For there is faithful love with the LORD,
and with him is redemption in abundance.

PSALM 130:7

Whenever I pulled into our driveway in the late fall, I'd feel emotional just seeing my camellia bush. That simple shrub has weathered many storms and taught me to hope when all hope seemed lost.

Years ago, on an October day after my infant son Paul died, a friend brought over a camellia bush which blooms every fall. I treasured that bush, so when we moved, I took it to our new home. We carefully dug around all the roots and planted it right by the front door. At first it looked gorgeous, but the heat of summer was too harsh, and the plant too traumatized from the move. Soon its leaves fell off, leaving a brittle mass of dry twigs.

But it was so connected with Paul that getting rid of it was unthinkable. So it sat there lifeless, reminding me that I have no control over what lives or dies.

Our landscaper knew nothing of our plant's history. To him it was just a dead bush. So one day when I was gone, he cut it down to the stump. When I asked about it, he said, "I'm sorry I didn't ask you first. But it was dead you know."

Yes. I knew. It was dead, and there was no point keeping it. All winter long, I mourned the barren space which seemed like a fitting metaphor for my life. It seemed irrational, but the ache was all too real. I didn't know why, but I felt that I had let Paul down. Why was this so important? Why did I cry every time I thought about it?

One spring day, glancing at the space by the door, I was stunned. Green leaves were covering the stump. Though the branches had been destroyed, the roots remained. When I could only see my loss, God was working for my good. Within a few weeks, a small bush had formed again. What I thought was dead was now alive.

I wept when I saw my camellia covered with blossoms in the fall. It represented hope to me. When we moved from that house a few years ago, I had to leave my beloved camellia bush behind because it had become too big to transplant. When I drove by my old home the following year, I was taken aback at the transformation. The camellia bush had been shaped into a tree that was covered with gorgeous white flowers, a focal point of the yard. No one would have believed that it had been cut to the ground and left for dead just a few years earlier. No one but God who knew all along what it would become.

God is always working, often when we see no signs of what He's doing. Nothing is beyond redemption. God makes pathways in the wilderness and creates rivers in the dry wasteland. And when all seems lost, redemption may be closer than we think.

———————

REFLECT: What in your life seems dead beyond restoration? What is keeping you from asking God to bring new life in this situation?

When All Hope Seems Lost

For many days neither sun nor stars appeared,
and the severe storm kept raging. Finally all
hope was fading that we would be saved.

ACTS 27:20

I was sinking into a dull depression. Nothing was good and life seemed gray.

My life had fallen apart, and there was no repairing it. Everywhere I turned, things were hard.

So much of my life had disintegrated. My husband had left our family, and our children decided that God wasn't real. They were angry and disillusioned, and my health was spiraling downward. I was struggling to even care for myself, let alone two adolescent daughters.

I was at one of the lowest points in my life. I was losing hope, like the apostle Paul's companions on their boat adrift at sea, convinced my situation would never change.

I was talking with some friends about how I was feeling. I didn't really want to talk, but I knew that talking to friends was important. Especially when I wanted to pull away.

Soon after we started, I couldn't speak anymore. I just sat there, crying.

After a long silence, one friend spoke. I will never forget her words.

"When I think of you and pray for you, I keep seeing this image. It's of the disciples and Jesus's mother Mary weeping at the foot of the cross. They are huddled together, trying to comfort one another and to make sense of what has happened, but it just doesn't make sense. The sky is black and all hope looks lost. Their dreams have died. It seems that nothing good will ever come from this. To them, this day, Good Friday, is the darkest day they've ever known. But the one thing that they do not know is . . . Easter is coming."

Easter is coming.

I could scarcely take in the words. As she finished speaking, I was filled with an indescribable peace.

Of course. Easter is coming. I stopped crying.

Her picture was arresting. As I imagined how the disciples and Mary must have felt, I felt a bond with them. They knew what it was like to feel desperate. Dreams shattered. Life ruined. Plans destroyed.

At that point they could only see part of the picture. The part they were living at the time. That's all they had.

I couldn't see how God could bring anything good out of my situation. But as I let her words wash over me, I realized that my story wasn't over yet. God was not finished. God does miraculous things. Even when all hope seems lost.

———————

PRAY: Lord, You know my heart. You see my anguish and my grief. You understand the devastation and ruin. Standing at the foot of the cross, I release it all to You. And though my eyes are filled with tears and I cannot see clearly, I believe that *in You* my story is not over. Help me to keep trusting.

Dealing with Regret

Regret. People don't talk about regret very much, but it can be an unexpectedly big part of suffering. It's painful to look back on the things we did, wishing we could replay what happened. We wonder if we had made a different choice, seen things a bit differently, known what we know now, would things have taken a different trajectory.

One of my major regrets is that I didn't take our son Paul to the ER sooner. When I called a high school friend who was a pediatric cardiologist, he suggested we take Paul to the hospital. The changes his doctor had made with his medicine just didn't seem right to him. This was Friday night; Paul was doing well with no symptoms, and I assumed I could wait till Monday. I thought a few days wouldn't matter. But in a few days my son was dead.

Then there were the regrets when I was a single parent and would drive to a nearby grocery parking lot to cry and vent my frustrations. Kristi would often get right in my face, and when I was on the verge of breaking down in angry tears, I'd leave before I retaliated. While my actions may sound understandable, they hurt Kristi deeply. She'd stand at the door begging me not to go. I always went anyway.

I didn't know that she felt abandoned by her dad and now abandoned by me as she stood sobbing at the door. I didn't know that she was so lonely at school that she ate her lunch in the bathroom stall every day. I didn't know that the pain she was dishing out was erupting from all the pain she was holding inside.

If only I'd known. Made different choices. Cared less about myself and my comfort. Yet at this point I can't change any of them. I'm guessing you have regrets of your own. If you roll your regrets over in your head as I do, remember that God is sovereign even over our mistakes. And He forgives us when we confess our sins. We do not need to carry the burden of all the things we've done wrong or the mistakes we've made, or the "what if I hads" or the "I should haves" many of us carry.

The gospel sets us free from dwelling on our mistakes, refusing to forgive ourselves. God calls us instead to dwell on His grace and forgiveness. That doesn't mean we won't have regrets, but it does mean we don't need to carry them with us. The Lord invites us all to lay them at the cross knowing that Christ's blood covers them. To ask for forgiveness for the things we've done wrong. To make restoration for the mistakes that we've made. And to trust God with the rest.

———————

REFLECT: What regrets are you holding onto? What do you need to let go of?

42

When Life-Giving Bread
Tastes Like Stale Crackers

Open my eyes, that I may behold
wondrous things out of your law.
PSALM 119:18 ESV

Yesterday when I opened my Bible, I found myself thinking about everything else but what I was reading: my worries about one of my daughters, a new health problem, an unexpected home repair. With those concerns in the back of my mind, I found my thoughts drifting from the passage in front of me to what the day might hold.

I "checked off" that part of the reading and flipped to the next section when I realized I hadn't absorbed a word. Or even felt like I had spoken to God or listened to Him. When I realized I was just going through the motions, I stopped and prayed using the WORD acronym below. This is a prayer that turns me to God, reminding me that the Bible is a spiritual book and I need God's help to understand it.

This is my WORD prayer:

W—Waken my ears to listen to Your voice (Isa. 50:4).

O—Open my eyes to see truth and understand it (Ps. 119:18).

R—Reveal my sin and Your ways (Ps. 25:8; Heb. 4:12).

D—Direct my heart to Your love and to worship (2 Thess. 3:5; Ps. 106:1).

I came up with that acronym because I want to hear God speak to me through His Word but also in the silence. I once heard someone say, "God is always talking to us, but are we listening?" I want to listen. Intently. God can show me what I cannot see or understand without His wisdom. Through reading, I want God to convict me of my sin, to help me understand myself, and to show me His ways. Finally, I want to recognize that I am God's beloved, which is written throughout the Bible. And truly understanding His love will always lead me to worship.

After praying, I started intentionally looking at the Scripture, writing thoughts in my journal and in the Bible margins. There was so much to glean in what I'd carelessly skimmed. So much to offer in prayer and in praise. So much to gain when my goal was not just finishing. I prayed the Scripture, asking God for understanding, not to increase my knowledge but to fellowship with Him. In my hurry to read, I could have missed the treasures

God had for me. That's not always the case, as some mornings my reading feels more like eating stale crackers than life-giving bread. But usually when I ask God to show me something from His Word, praying Psalm 119:18, I'm amazed at all I see.

WRITE: On an index card, write out the acrostic WORD with the references. Consider keeping it in your Bible so you can pray it prior to reading the Word. Invite the Lord to meet you in His Word.

43

Can We Find Joy When We've Lost Everything?

*Though the fig tree should not blossom, nor fruit be
on the vines, the produce of the olive fail and the fields
yield no food, the flock be cut off from the fold and
there be no herd in the stalls, yet I will rejoice in the
LORD; I will take joy in the God of my salvation.*

HABAKKUK 3:17–18 ESV

When I discovered that termites had eaten the supports of
our garage, I had no words. It had been a year of continual loss, and I couldn't take another thing. Or so I thought. I felt like God was stripping everything away. Nothing felt firm, not even the foundations of our house. I was trying to find joy, but all I felt was despair.

Have you ever felt that way? If you have, you understand why those last verses of Habakkuk are so shocking. This passage is about losing everything. Having nothing to eat. Nothing to sell. Nothing to build a life on.

Habakkuk is not looking past the circumstances of today toward a better day when God will redeem everything. He is asserting that even in the middle of this terrible situation, he will find joy in God. Even though nothing around him looks good, and there are no signs of anything changing.

This unflinching honesty is why Habakkuk 3 is so comforting. Habakkuk shows us that joy is not rooted in our circumstances. We can have joy even in sorrow. And sometimes our joy can deepen in sorrow.

How is that even possible? How do you have joy when life is in shambles? How does anyone rejoice when life is falling apart?

It's not easy. It does not happen naturally. What happens naturally in my heart is resentment, frustration, envying others, and wondering why God hasn't delivered me yet. So I can't just let my natural tendencies take over. I will fixate on what is wrong and what's been taken away. I must deliberately take my eyes off myself and my problems and fix them firmly on Jesus.

I'm trying to do that. And when I do, my body relaxes and my perspective changes. I experience joy in simply being with Christ, poring over His Word, talking to Him constantly, sensing His presence everywhere I go. It's one thing to hang a plaque on the wall about trusting God; it's another thing to live and breathe it.

Finding joy in God alone, completely depending and relying on Him, made little sense to me as a young believer when much of my life seemed idyllic. Yet as life grew more difficult, I began to understand what Habakkuk was talking about. There were years when every day was filled with struggle and pain, when nothing I did was successful or bore fruit. And in those years I understood true joy.

Habakkuk 3 is an exquisite example of this joy. A joy not based on the assumption that tomorrow will be a better day but rather based on being with Jesus, now and forever.

———————

REFLECT: Where does your life feel barren right now? Are you able to rejoice, like Habakkuk, in the face of loss today? Why or why not?

44

Does Your Situation Feel Impossible?

For nothing will be impossible with God.

LUKE 1:37

For me to believe that a situation can change, I want to see signs that it's already changing. But God doesn't always work that way. Sometimes it's slow gradual work, and other times it's miraculous and unexpected, when we've almost given up.

I prayed for years about a situation, read books, begged God, and asked people to pray with me, but nothing seemed to make a difference.

After years of struggle, I was reenergized by a conference speaker who mentioned praying on her face every day for something she longed for. I decided to do it. So day after day I would lie prostrate on the carpet and cry out to God. I pleaded with God for wisdom and for a miracle. I read the psalms. I implored God like the centurion who asked Jesus to heal his servant by just saying the word. I prayed throughout the day as well. Whenever I was frustrated, I would talk to God about it.

I felt a spark of hope when I read, "God . . . gives life to the dead and calls things into existence that do not exist" (Rom. 4:17). I didn't need to see progress for God to work in a supernatural way. He could simply speak it into existence. And one day He did.

There may be something in your life that may seem dead right now. Your dreams. Your health. Your relationships. Keep asking God for the desires of your heart. Believe that He can bring a miracle. Keep praying and asking. Like a child who tugs on her father's sleeve, continually asking whenever she thinks of her request, not worried that she will wear him out, you too can keep asking God.

God may be about to do something miraculous. Joseph had no idea that one day he'd be released from prison and become the second in command of all of Egypt. Elizabeth had no idea when she was past childbearing years that she would give birth to John, the forerunner of the Messiah.

These Scriptures have reassured me to keep praying, knowing that God can do anything:

- Jeremiah 32:27: "Look, I am the LORD, the God over every creature. Is anything too difficult for me?"
- Proverbs 21:1: "A king's heart is like channeled water in the LORD's hand: He directs it wherever he chooses."

- Hebrews 11:3: "By faith we understand that the universe was created by the word of God, so that what is seen was made from things that are not visible."

Maybe today you are facing something that feels impossible. Perhaps it's hard to believe that it could ever change. Maybe you're tired of praying and can't see any way out. Don't despair. Keep talking to God and leaning into Him. God is watching and listening and can move heaven and earth for you. All things are God's servants, and He can redirect anyone's heart simply by saying the word. For nothing is impossible with God.

MEMORIZE: Write today's verse on an index card. Put it where you'll see it regularly so you can memorize it.

Can We Be Honest about Our Pain?

*"I went away full, and the LORD has brought
me back empty. Why call me Naomi, when
the LORD has testified against me and the
Almighty has brought calamity upon me?"*
RUTH 1:21 ESV

I don't know what to do with all my anger and disappointment. I can't tell God how I feel because I don't know where that will take me. And if I tell anyone else, it sounds like I don't trust God."

A friend admitted that to me over coffee, whispering so the people at the table beside us wouldn't hear. She had been through years of heartache and had seemingly weathered it all with a smile. But underneath it, she felt like she was dying.

I understand that thinking. For years, I thought the most God-honoring attitude was cheerful acceptance, which meant looking happy all the time. Even when I was confused and angry.

Even when my heart was breaking. And especially when I was around people who didn't know Christ.

But I have since learned the importance of honesty and the beauty of lament in suffering. Lament is crying out to God, even screaming in our pain, while trusting in His goodness. I've found that my honest lament highlights the gospel more than stoicism ever could. When I lament, people see that God wants to know them, that they can be real with Him, and that Christians aren't pretending to have joy, putting on a happy face when they feel sad.

The book of Ruth shows us the power of lament. Ruth witnessed her mother-in-law Naomi's honesty firsthand. Ruth saw Naomi's faith hold fast, even after the death of her husband and her two sons. And behind Naomi's faith, she saw the God who heard Naomi's lament and didn't condemn her for it, even as Naomi spoke frankly about her disappointment with God.

Lamenting to a god would have been foreign to Ruth, who was a Moabite. No one would have dared complain to pagan gods who even demanded child sacrifices to be appeased. But Ruth saw a completely different God as she watched Naomi. Naomi trusted God enough to tell Him how she felt, refusing to give up and walk away in anger.

After watching Naomi, Ruth gave up everything to follow her God. She saw His faithfulness through Naomi, a woman who had seen unspeakable tragedy yet continued to pursue God.

Like Naomi, our authenticity can draw others to God as it allows them to be honest too. God knows our tendency to either pretend everything is okay while we suffocate on the inside or to walk away from God believing He doesn't care. Lamenting invites God into our pain so that we can know His comfort and others can see that our faith is real. Our faith is not a facade we erect to convince ourselves and others that pain doesn't hurt, but it is rather an oak tree that can withstand the storms of doubt and pain in our lives and grow stronger through them.

REFLECT: When have you been tempted to put on a mask on your suffering to "protect" others' opinion of God? And how can you choose, today, to invite God into your pain through lament? Psalm 13 is a wonderful model for our own lament as David begins with: "How long, Lord? Will you forget me forever? How long will you hide your face from me?" Consider offering your own lament to God using the format of this psalm by journaling, talking to a friend, or simply sitting with God.

46

God Has Not Forgotten You

*"Can a woman forget her nursing child, or lack
compassion for the child of her womb?
Even if these forget, yet I will not forget you."*
Isaiah 49:15

G od has not forgotten you."

As I heard those words from a speaker years ago, I broke down. Unexpected tears streamed down my face as I faced how lonely and abandoned I'd been feeling. Each day was harder than the one before, and I wondered why God hadn't rescued me. I felt like He had forgotten about me.

After her message, I felt stirred to look past my situation, to look at the character of God, and to trust that He was working. Her words refocused me on these bedrock truths:

1. *God will be with me.* The assurance that God is with us is the most precious gift we have in suffering. As Christians we know that God is always with us and that there is nowhere we

can flee from His presence, but actually sensing God's presence and comfort is different. His presence has given me joy when I was discouraged, refreshed me when I was weary, and removed my fears when I was in a dark valley.

2. *God has a good purpose for my suffering.* If my suffering was meaningless, I couldn't have withstood it. I would have felt crushed, bitter, ripped off, full of regret and doubt, wondering whether my bad decision, or someone else's, had kept me from the successful life I'd longed for. Life would have felt unfair and even cruel.

By faith, we know that God has a reason and purpose for our pain—perhaps thousands of reasons—and they are all for our good, regardless of how it looks or feels on the surface.

3. *My pain will end one day.* No matter what pain we are going through, if we are in Christ, we know that it won't last forever. Our suffering is momentary as we consider it in light of eternity. God will make all things new; we have endless and painless joy awaiting us in heaven.

Some of us may get deliverance in this life, and tomorrow may bring redemption beyond our wildest dreams. But either way, if we are His, our pain will surely and completely end whether on earth or in heaven.

If you are struggling today, remember God has not forgotten you. He has engraved you on the palms of His hands. He is using your suffering and pain in ways you would not believe if someone told you. And after you have suffered a little while, He will Himself restore and establish you.

PRAY: Lord, You know the ways I have felt forgotten by You. I know that You are with me, there's a purpose for my suffering, and my pain will end one day. But right now, none of those things feel real. Show me how to rest in Your love.

The Mystery of Healing

Heal me, LORD, and I will be healed; save me,
and I will be saved, for you are my praise.

JEREMIAH 17:14

Healing is a bit of a puzzle to me. I know that God can heal, that He still heals people today, that prayer is part of healing, and yet not all who pray in faith are healed. Not everyone has gotten that memo, as I still have people stop me in grocery stores, ask me what is wrong, and declare they can heal me right there in the Walmart checkout line. Even after the cashier has started ringing up my rotisserie chicken.

Sometimes there's a crowd watching. When my daughter Kristi was in a Christian basketball program, her teenage coach proclaimed he was going to heal me. He prayed loudly and confidently, but when I wasn't healed, he sauntered away as the other parents and players looked at us with pity. It seemed more about his pride than it was about me.

I felt that way in college when I went to a campus ministry meeting that featured a traveling faith healer. When I walked in, the auditorium was already packed. After the healer gave a short message, individual conversations erupted as everyone who lined up received immediate healing from earaches, migraines, and stomach problems. But when a ministry leader urged me to the front, the room fell silent.

The faith healer tried numerous times, touching my shoulders and legs and claiming my healing. But when he'd ask me to walk, my limp was as pronounced. He frowned and finally said something like, "I need to ask you, do you have the faith to be healed?" I said that I thought so, but he responded, "I know I can heal everyone who has enough faith, but I don't think you do. You should pray and ask God to give you that faith. I'll be doing a healing service tomorrow night, and if you pray and get the faith you need, you'll be healed then. I'm sure of it."

Someone helped me off the stage as he turned to the next person. I was mortified.

Late that night I penned a journal entry that began with, "I'm so confused, and I don't know what to think. . . . If you want me to be healed, Lord, give me the faith."

I know God does not promise us healing on this side of heaven, but I also have seen Him heal, not based on the faith of the healed but on the will of God. I do not claim to know why God heals some physically while others He does not, but I know it is not due to the size of their faith but the astounding power of God. I too have received miraculous physical healing. When I was young, I used ankle braces. The doctors had just told my parents I would never walk without them when a faith healer prayed over me. I haven't worn braces since, and the doctors to this day are astounded.

I don't understand why or when or through whom God chooses to heal, but I do know God has done a deeper healing in my life because of my disability. He has taught me to trust Him. He's refined my character and given me joy in Him apart from my circumstances. And those gifts have become far more precious than any physical healing.

REFLECT: How has God used what is not healed in you to do a different kind of work in your life or another's? What gifts have you received on the journey?

48

I Never Want to Forgive at First

"For if you forgive others their offenses, your heavenly Father will forgive you as well."
MATTHEW 6:14

Even the word *forgiveness* can make me bristle. I wonder if you feel the same way. I immediately think of past wounds that have barely stopped bleeding, and I see no good reason to let go of them. What I'd rather do is dwell and replay all the cruel and unkind things others have said and done to me, plotting my retaliation if only in my mind.

I vividly remember sitting in my counselor's office, talking about my ex-husband's affair. When the counselor mentioned forgiveness, I was furious. I wasn't going to offer him a "get out of jail free" card after all I had suffered. Just hearing the word made me angry. Why should I forgive, especially when he hadn't even acknowledged all the damage he'd done?

But as my counselor unpacked the biblical principles of forgiveness, I realized I hadn't fully understood what forgiveness meant. Forgiveness is not saying that what the person did was okay or minimizing the offense. God forgave our sins because they were so monumental we could never make up for them. And God calls us to forgive others, just as we've been forgiven by Him.

So I decided to forgive, first saying the words and then asking God to change my heart. I realized that forgiveness was a process, not just a one-time event. I wrote down all the ways my ex-husband had hurt me, all he had taken from me, and as new things came to mind, I kept asking God to help me forgive those as well. As I did, I saw that through forgiveness, God was cleaning out the poison I had been pouring into my wounds. And I began to heal.

Years later, as I was organizing an old cabinet, I found a "You Are Special" plate with our last name in big letters that I'd painted when our children were young. I wouldn't use it again so I decided to send it to my ex-husband and his wife so they could use it with their children. As I packed it up, I prayed that they would use it for generations, a symbol of how God's love and forgiveness can change our hearts.

While it may sound like I'm an expert at forgiveness, I still resist forgiving people who have hurt me. So I know how difficult it can be. Perhaps the wound for you is still fresh, and you need time to process all that's happened. Or maybe you've been holding on to bitterness for a long time, and God is nudging you to let it go. If that's you, I encourage you to pray. To trust God.

To forgive your offender. You won't regret it. You may be amazed at how quickly God begins to flood your life with the joy and peace you lost.

WRITE: Ask God to show you anything that is keeping you stuck today. Write out specifically how you've been hurt and all the layers you can think of. Then listen to God. Ask God for the strength to release the offense by forgiving the other. Jot down any resistance you notice inside. Continue to listen, and note the words God speaks to your heart.

49

What's the Point
of Suffering That
No One Sees?

*Therefore, since we also have such a large cloud
of witnesses surrounding us, let us lay aside every
hindrance and the sin that so easily ensnares us. Let
us run with endurance the race that lies before us.*

Hebrews 12:1

D o you ever wonder if there's any point to suffering in obscurity?

For years I questioned whether my private suffering had meaning. I understood that public suffering inspired people to see the value of God. But unseen suffering seemed pointless.

Nothing could have been further from the truth.

I've since learned that, instead of being insignificant, our private suffering carries massive significance, with far-reaching eternal consequences. Our suffering is, in fact, never private because everything we do and say is being watched by the unseen world, a world of angels and demons, of powers and principalities, of a great cloud of witnesses, and our triune God Himself. While this may sound unnerving to some, knowing we're surrounded by all these unseen spectators has inspired me to press on through my own pain.

We are all on a giant battleground, where angels and demons are craning their necks to see what they can learn about God through us. They are watching to see how God helps us, how His presence dispels our fears, and how He inspires our worship. This isn't sci-fi fantasy or some reassuring myth designed to ease our pain and loneliness. No, the stunning truth that we are constantly being watched is firmly grounded in Scripture, in the Old and New Testament.

Joni Eareckson Tada recalled lying awake in bed at 2:00 a.m., nauseous from chemo and wondering if it was all worth it. She remembered Ephesians 3:10, realizing, "Something dynamic and electrifying is abuzz in my dark room. The unseen world in the spirit realm, all the heavenly hosts, including powers and principalities, they're watching me. They are listening to me. And as I respond, they are learning about God and His character through me—little me. I can't tell you how many times I've been able to press on because I know my life is on display."[26]

As this hidden world watches us, they see God's grace sustain us, His power deliver us, and His comfort encourage us. They see us glorify God when we are unfairly accused and choose to respond with grace. They notice when we are worried about a loved one and choose to trust God. They pay attention when we are racked with pain and choose to praise God through our tears. These choices all matter because a heavenly host is watching and our faithfulness in trial may be shaking the universe.

So don't believe the lie that your suffering doesn't matter, that no one is watching, and that there's no point to your faithfulness. While it may seem like you're suffering alone in a dark room, you're actually on an enormous stage, perhaps akin to a jumbotron, with innumerable eyewitnesses. So let's press on knowing that our lives are on display.

REFLECT: How does knowing that a cloud of witnesses is watching and cheering you on encourage you in what you are going through?

The Reason Not to Fear

*"Haven't I commanded you: be strong and
courageous? Do not be afraid or discouraged, for
the LORD your God is with you wherever you go."*
JOSHUA 1:9

I went out of state to college, despite being afraid of how I would manage the sprawling campus. Many of the historic buildings had no railings in the front, and for one class I'd regularly ask strangers who were sitting on the long marble staircase for help. But one day, it was pouring rain, and everything was deserted.

I stood outside, frustrated, tears welling up. By now I was drenched and didn't have the strength to walk home for fear I would fall. There wasn't even anything I could lean on. I muttered, "God, You promised to take care of me. Where are You? I need Your help. Please come quickly!"

As I was praying, someone suddenly appeared, a stranger I had never seen before. He had a huge golf umbrella and asked if I needed help up the steps. I nodded and he quickly got me inside. When I turned around to thank him, he was gone. I didn't even see him walking down the steps.

That day God showed me that He would be with me wherever I went. That's why I never need to fear.

The most repeated command in the Bible is, "Do not be afraid." It's not a hammer commanding us not to fear but a tender invitation to trust. Especially when it's combined with the most repeated promise, "I am with you." This is the reason not to fear—the Lord is with us.

Through the years, knowing God is with me has given me courage when I was afraid. It hasn't always eliminated my fears, especially when I'm not looking for God, not actively searching for signs that He is near. But when God reminds me to call out to Him, I often say like the psalmist, "Show me a sign of your goodness" (Ps. 86:17).

The storms in your new life may have brought many unknowns. Maybe your small boat is being buffeted by the wind and the waves. When Jesus sent the disciples out on a tumultuous night, they were terrified when He came to them walking on the water. Jesus reassured them saying, "Have courage! It is I. Don't be afraid" (Mark 6:50).

I wonder if Jesus is saying that to you today. That you can take courage because He is with you. There is no need to fear. God has been to the future and knows what is there. And He will give you all that you need to face it. He knows that your greatest need isn't healing or answers or friends or certainty. Your greatest need is Him.

MEMORIZE: Write today's verse on an index card. Put it where you'll see it regularly so you can memorize it.

51

When We Need
the Comfort of Others

*Now when Job's three friends . . . heard about all
this adversity that had happened to him, each of
them came from his home. They met together to
go and sympathize with him and comfort him.*

JOB 2:11

The day after Paul died, I was thankful our house was filled with people. Friends bringing casseroles, stopping by, coming to grieve with us. I wanted companionship. Someone to sit with me. Someone to put human flesh on God's comfort.

Having people around when I'm struggling has always been important to me, but it felt slightly unspiritual. I felt that God alone should be sufficient to meet my needs and I shouldn't need anyone else. Then I saw it. In His darkest moments, in the garden of Gethsemane, Jesus wanted His friends to watch and wait with Him. Jesus didn't ask His disciples to accompany Him when He was communing with His Father. He often arose early in the morning to be with God by Himself. But we see that in His hour of desperation, when He was facing unspeakable agony, He asked His friends to be with Him.

Clearly this longing was not sinfully weak or needy. It did not reflect a lack of trust in God or a fragile faith. It was simply human. God incarnate longed for fellowship. Because God created us to live in community.

In the same way, we often long for presence in our suffering. Being cared for from a distance is not enough. We aren't looking for answers to our deepest questions or solutions to our pressing problems. Sitting with a friend is a huge gift, though everyone may want something different from a friend's presence. Some may communicate little, while others are flooded with words.

No matter how we process, no one is requesting a deluge of words in response. We don't want to be fixed or corrected; we just want to be seen and known. We want the freedom to be ourselves as we figure out what that means.

I still remember a friend who stopped by frequently after Paul's death. She rarely spoke and mostly sat unobtrusively. I loved having her there. I didn't have to make conversation, but I knew she'd listen if I wanted to talk.

Author Joe Bayly had a similar experience after burying his second son. Bayly says,

> I was sitting, torn by grief. Someone came and talked to me of God's dealings, of why it happened, of hope beyond the grave. He talked constantly; he said things I knew were true. I was

unmoved, except to wish he'd go away. He finally did.

Another came and sat beside me. He didn't talk. He didn't ask leading questions. He just sat beside me for an hour or more, listened when I said something, answered briefly, prayed simply, left. I was moved. I was comforted. I hated to see him go.[27]

REFLECT: When you suffer, are you naturally drawn to isolation or to the company of others? When you've suffered, who have been the ones who've embodied God's steadfast faithful presence with you?

52

The Despair
of the Wilderness

*He found him in a desolate land, in a barren,
howling wilderness; he surrounded him, cared for
him, and protected him as the pupil of his eye.*

<small>DEUTERONOMY 32:10</small>

Years ago, I went kicking and screaming into the wilderness. My husband had left, and my life was ripping apart at the seams. At times I felt that it had completely unraveled. I was unsettled and afraid, hoping this situation and all my related fears and uncertainty would quickly resolve.

At first, I was sure this was a detour. This couldn't be where God wanted me. But when days turned into weeks, which turned into months and then years, I realized I had to figure out how to live in this barren place. Before that, my definition of the good life had little to do with God and more to do with pleasant circumstances. God was an extra bonus to deliver all that I wanted and felt I deserved.

In the wilderness, God dismantled my comfortable life. It came when I was feeling particularly confident. This is not unusual; Elijah went into the wilderness right after his defeat of the prophets of Baal. Moses led Israel into the wilderness after God parted the Red Sea, delivering them out of slavery. Yet the contrast from where I'd just been made it harder to notice anything good. I wondered why God had brought me there and if He was going to leave me there. I was terrified.

It was the lowest emotional point of my life. I was discouraged, looking for security and assurance, while Satan kept whispering that God had abandoned me. Everything looked empty, and I wondered if God even cared. I was tired of waiting. Tired of having my life on hold. Tired of being dependent on God for everything.

But there was no way out, no end that I could see, so I learned to survive in the wilderness. I leaned into God. I persevered. I prayed and I cried. I lamented and cried some more. I read Scripture to give me hope. I waited for God as I relied on His promises.

If you are in the wilderness right now, don't give up. Press into God with your discouragement and disillusionment. Ask Him to provide for your needs. Tell Him everything on your heart, especially your fears and doubts. Don't hold back. Then look around. God is showing you things you can't learn elsewhere. He is caring for you and providing for your needs. As you recognize He is with you in this desolate place, it can tether your heart to Jesus like nothing else can.

You may not feel you're learning anything in the wilderness. Maybe you feel like you're just surviving. But trust that God is doing something in what looks like a wasteland. He's reshaping your heart and preparing you for what comes next, perhaps a time of unprecedented fruitfulness. And through every difficult moment, every never-ending day and every sleepless night, He's transforming you into His image.

———————

PRAY: God, I need You. I know what it is to be in the wilderness. I know what it is to be tired. I know what it is to be lonely. God, I have nothing but You; help me trust that You're all I need. Reshape my heart and make me ready for what You have prepared for me.

53

I Am Letting the Tears Fall

My eyes are worn out from crying.
LORD, I cry out to you all day long;
I spread out my hands to you.

PSALM 88:9

L ike lament psalms, my desperate words don't always end
with light. Sometimes I just have to let the tears fall. This is
one of those laments:

> Lord, I can't stop crying. As I reflect on the week,
> it all feels like too much. Much more than I can
> handle or process. This week I started using a
> wheelchair again because of the crazy awful nerve
> pain I just can't escape. My new orthopedic sur-
> geon seems indifferent, like I'm just another whin-
> ing patient, or maybe he's just busy and clinical.
>
> I cherished being able to walk, so when a
> friend asked how I was doing using the wheel-
> chair, I didn't know how to respond. I wasn't

sure how honest to be—with her or even myself.
I know hopeful and holy words, but my heart is
often disconnected from them. I'm afraid to voice
my fears, to myself or others, because I feel like
I'm stepping into the abyss. So I just block it all
out.

My hair has been falling out by the handfuls.
I've lost more than 60 percent of my once thick
curly hair. When I saw myself on a Zoom call
recently, I cried. It may seem like a superficial
problem, but I'm tired of dying to the things that
are important to me.

I'm failing everyone. When we visit grand-
children, I can't do anything with them. I can't
pull them onto my lap, play fun games with them,
really do anything. I feel useless. I wonder if they
see me as someone who loves them.

My stomach issues have been going on for a
year. At times they get so awful but I just can't go
to another doctor's appointment and have them
run more tests and have no idea what it is. Lord,
I keep praying, but You have not provided any
answers.

I'm processing it all, not trying to rush past
the pain or tie a theological bow on it. These are
hard losses in a long series of losses. I'm tired and
discouraged, and the future feels frightening. I
wonder when my daily physical needs will be

more than Joel can manage by himself. What will happen then? Who will fix my hair? Put on my makeup? Brush my teeth? I'm scared of being a burden, and I hate asking for everything.

Oh God, I can't do this. I need You to rescue me. To give me answers when all I have are questions. To give me peace because I feel anxious. To give me hope because I feel hopeless. I know You will. But today, maybe I just need to sit in the hard. I know You are with me, but I can't feel Your presence now.

Lord, I know You are good. I know You will never leave me. I know You have good plans for me. I know my help will come from the Lord who made heaven and earth. And I know that You will give me the grace I need each day. While I know all these things, today still feels impossibly hard.

It's dark outside. I'm staring out the window, watching for the morning.

Are you also watching for the morning, even as you're sitting in the darkest night?

———————

REFLECT: What is the hard desperate prayer you need to share with God today?

54

What Story Are You Telling Yourself?

Blessed be the LORD, for he has wondrously shown
his faithful love to me in a city under siege.
PSALM 31:21

When I was a child, I was on a long flight with my mother and sister. We hit severe turbulence, and the plane started wildly swinging, dropping rapidly without warning, as countless people pulled out their airsick bags. Everyone around us was panicking as the flight attendants took their seats. People wondered if the pilot was losing control or if the plane was about to crash. You could cut the tension and the fear that hung in the air.

My sister and I, on the other hand, were blissfully free of any anxiety. We loved the plane ride because it felt just like a roller coaster. We didn't know there was anything to fear, and so we were unafraid. At one point I turned to my mom and said, "Isn't

God nice making the plane go up and down, up and down like that? It's fun!"

Isn't God nice? I'm guessing no one else on the plane was thinking that in the midst of the chaos. But my sister and I had no context for what was happening, and so we were able to just take in the moment without worrying about the next one. We accepted the precipitous drops in altitude for what they were without attaching any meaning to them.

My friend Raquel recently commented, "We are afraid of storms when we're in the boat because we are afraid of what might happen next. Even if we know we're in the boat with Christ. Can we get into Christ's boat in the storm, experiencing the wind like a laughing child?"

Of course, the storms in our lives don't feel breezy as they descend on us. They can be terrifying. Much of our fear is not what is happening in the moment but our interpretation of what's going on. We wonder where it is leading. We tell ourselves we are in danger, that nothing good will come in the end. We convince ourselves that our lives are out of control and could crash at any time. We doubt God's goodness and power and give in to fear.

What you tell yourself in your suffering is not trivial. It will profoundly affect your experience because suffering is spiritual warfare. Paul Tripp says that suffering is not just a matter of the body; it is also a matter of the heart. And what you are telling yourself in your pain is critical because "your suffering is more powerfully shaped by what's in your heart than by what's in your body or in the world around you."[28]

Those words have been so helpful for me, as I pay attention to what I am telling myself in my suffering. I need to remember the gospel of God's grace—the reality of His presence, power, and provision as I lean into the goodness of God.

WRITE: What are you telling yourself in your suffering? List specifically what thoughts come to you. If you could look at the situation from God's perspective instead of your own, what do you imagine you might see?

55

Is Your Faith Greater Than Your Fear?

*Your way went through the sea and your path through
the vast water, but your footprints were unseen.*

PSALM 77:19

L et your faith be greater than your fear. For years, those
words were on a plaque in my office to remind me to trust
God when I was afraid. I would stare at the sign, and just reading it gave me courage. But even more than reading the plaque, I
learned that when I'm afraid of the future, I need to start talking
to myself. Here's what I do:

1. Remember God's faithfulness. Reciting God's promises,
His past faithfulness, and His character will help us trust Him
with our fears. When I'm discouraged or afraid, I read Psalms. I
recently reread Psalm 77, one I turn to again and again. Psalms
were originally read aloud, and many were songs like this one,
which is addressed "to the choirmaster" (ESV). I imagine that as

the people heard and sang it, they mentally inserted their own experiences as they put their voices to the words.

God calls us to remember all that He has done for us. The Israelites did that regularly, reminding one another of how God redeemed His people, parted the Red Sea, and worked wonders among them.

2. Follow your fear and see where it takes you. Psalm 46 shows us that even if the world is falling apart, we don't have to be afraid. We can be still and know God's presence. For me, knowing I might eventually be a quadriplegic terrifies me. But when I'm able to verbalize my fear, I think of my friend Joni Eareckson Tada, who has been a quadriplegic for decades and yet lives in joyful dependence on Jesus.

3. Trust that God will give you the grace you need when you need it. God will give you all you need today, and He will do that tomorrow too (Matt. 6:34). Remember that God will supply all your needs (Phil. 4:19).

4. Remember that nothing comes into your life that has not passed through God's loving hands first. And if God has permitted it, He will use it both for your good and for His glory (Rom. 8:28).

5. Remember that God is with you. He will never fail you or forsake you, and He will fight for you. No matter what you face, you won't walk through it alone (Deut. 3:22; Heb. 13:5b–6).

6. Keep your mind and your thoughts on the Lord (Isa. 26:3; Rom. 8:6; Phil. 4:8–9).

7. Pray. Tell God your fears. Seek the Lord. Let Him know what you need, and stay in constant conversation with Him (2 Chron. 20:3; Phil. 4:6–7).

No matter what happens, Jesus will be with us. We do not know the future, but the Lord does. He already knows tomorrow and is giving us all we need today to face whatever will happen.

———————

PRACTICE: What fears of the future are you holding onto? Choose one of the suggestions above; read and pray through the verses that accompany that step you choose.

56

How God's Word
Delivered Me from the Pit

*My life is down in the dust; give
me life through your word.*

PSALM 119:25

I discovered the power of God's Word in the pit of despair.

It was as if I had been caught up in a whirlwind—one that picked me up from my happy, secure life and threw me into a dark well. For days, I sat there alone, wondering if I had the strength to go on or if I even wanted to. I wondered if God's promises were true or if they would fail me as everything else had.

I was drawn to Psalm 119, looking for hope and light. I remember when I found it. Sobbing, I read verse 25: "My life is down in the dust; give me life through your word." This was how I felt. My life was in the dust, and I couldn't see a way out. I felt wrung out beyond my strength and wondered if anything could revive me. I cried out to God to give me life through His Word.

Just saying those words sparked something in me. I felt a glimmer of hope. I reread Psalm 119:82 with renewed interest and saw how it highlighted the gift of Scripture. When I needed words of grief and comfort, I repeated David's questions like, "My eyes grow weary looking for what you have promised; I ask, 'When will you comfort me?'"

I was revived as I repeated His promises, knowing I could trust them. I repeated Psalm 119:25 daily in my discouragement, and God met me. Everywhere I looked, I found hope, exactly in the Scripture bookmarked for the day. I approached my Bible reading with a different mindset—with anticipation, not a sense of obligation. I trusted that God would give me something to sustain me, so I read with purpose. Sometimes I had to dig to find the treasure. As John Piper said, "Raking is easy, but all you get is leaves; digging is hard, but you might find diamonds."[29]

I'd spent years having quiet times—some of them fruitful, some of them magnificent, many of them just perfunctory. Skimming the surface was my default, and a verse needed to jump out for me to pay attention to it. But now I expected to find what I needed for the day in God's Word. And I looked until I found it. I was the persistent widow, the merchant looking for pearls. God Himself was going to meet me. God was going to teach me. God was going to comfort me. His Word became my only constant, an immovable rock I could stand on when most of my life felt like shifting sand.

Those days changed my life, and I see Scripture differently. And it all began with a simple prayer borne out of desperation. I still pray this verse when I'm struggling, and God always answers.

MEMORIZE: Write today's verse on an index card. Put it where you'll see it regularly so you can memorize it.

57

Lighten My Load
or Strengthen My Back

"I relieved his shoulder from the burden; his
hands were freed from carrying the basket."
PSALM 81:6

He gives strength to the faint and
strengthens the powerless.
ISAIAH 40:29

T he words "Lighten my load or strengthen my back" were
pinned to my bulletin board for years. I needed God to
either lighten the burdens I was carrying or to give me strength
to endure them. I repeated those words, trusting God to give me
what was best, knowing that He wants to relieve our burdens.
Some people, however, offer a different prayer, such as the one
attributed to Phillips Brooks, who said, "I do not pray for a
lighter load, but a stronger back."[30] That certainly sounds more

holy than my words, and maybe I'm just a wimp, but I first ask God to take away the trial. Deep down, don't we all want God to fix our problems and take away our burdens, especially when we're feeling crushed?

Asking God to lighten our load and remove the trial we're facing is thoroughly biblical. People who were committed to God's will ask Him to take away their suffering. Jesus asked God to let the cup pass from Him, and Job begged God for deliverance. Paul pleaded three times with the Lord to remove his thorn, until the Lord told him that His grace was sufficient and that His power was made perfect in Paul's weakness (2 Cor. 12:8–9).

Our need. That's all we bring. The rest is all Him. We rely on God's grace. God's strength. God's power.

If God doesn't lighten our loads, we need Him to strengthen our backs. To strengthen us for what is happening now and whatever lies ahead. Strength doesn't make us self-sufficient; it helps us see how much we need God. We must rely on His grace, constantly asking God for help and strength.

I don't know if we are strengthened *in ourselves* for the next trial as much as we are better equipped for it. When God strengthens our back, we know how and where to get help. Our "help comes from the LORD, the Maker of heaven and earth" (Ps. 121:2). Rather than muscles of physical strength, perhaps the strength we get is muscle memory, reminding us to cry out to our God, who gives strength to the faint and strengthens the powerless (Isa. 40:29). On our own, we are often so utterly burdened and overwhelmed, beyond our strength, that we feel desperate.

Yet in our weakness and despair, we learn to rely on God, who raises the dead (2 Cor. 1:8–9).

God will give you the strength you need when you need it as you cry out to Him. You have that assurance. Yet the Lord encourages us to ask Him to lighten our loads—to ask, seek, and knock until we get an answer. Sometimes the answer is to remove the trial, and other times it is to strengthen us in it. So I will keep asking the Lord: *Will You lighten my load or strengthen my back?*

REFLECT: Looking over your life, where have you noticed that God has lightened your load or strengthened your back? And what is the heavy load you're carrying today?

58

If I Only Knew Why

Jesus answered him, "What I'm doing you don't realize now, but afterward you will understand."
JOHN 13:7

Have you ever been consumed with trying to understand why something happened? I have. I've been impacted by serious medical mistakes, and I've frequently wondered why.

I contracted polio long after it was supposedly eradicated. The doctor misdiagnosed my symptoms because she had never seen polio before. The wrong diagnosis led to widespread paralysis and a childhood spent largely in hospitals, marked by painful surgeries. And now, a deteriorating body.

I came to terms with my disability when I came to faith and saw God use it in my life, but then thirty years later, my son Paul died because of a doctor's mistake. This was harder to reconcile. It was completely unexpected and unfair. So my natural question was, "Why?" Why did this happen? If God was in control, why did He allow it? Why didn't He stop it?

I was sure that if I had an explanation, if I could understand why God permitted Paul's death to happen, if I just had a reason, then I could have accepted it more easily.

Are you being asked to trust God in a senseless situation—when the world feels like it has exploded, and you've been left to pick up the splintered fragments of your life?

God has asked us to go through the unthinkable. To trust Him in the dark and to accept His will when we don't understand. To believe He has a purpose when nothing makes sense. Unthinkable as it is, God keeps asking us to trust Him.

This invitation to trust is not what we want. We want to understand. We want to see. We want to agree. Accepting God's invitation takes faith, which we may possess in great measure when we are not in the furnace. But that faith wavers when the flames envelop us and our dreams fall apart.

But you may notice, as I did, that your questions only fuel your agitation. I eventually surrendered my desire to understand. Letting go of my need to know was the elusive key for which I had been searching. I learned that trusting, accepting, and submitting can transform us in our grief. Relinquishing your demand to understand may be what frees you.

While we think freedom will be found in answers, true freedom is actually found in surrender. We don't need to figure it out or understand the details. It doesn't need to make sense. We just need to trust God. Trust Him because He is infinitely wiser, more loving, and more purposeful than we are.

There is always a *why* to our pain. We may never understand it in this life, but this we can know: as we surrender our questions to Him, God will answer us with nothing less than Himself.

———————

PRAY: Lord, You know the questions in my heart. You know how I wrestle, asking, "Why?" And in the midst of my wonderings, I hear You inviting me to trust You in the dark. To accept what I cannot understand. Father, give me faith to trust You in what seems senseless. I surrender all to You. Meet me in the darkness.

In the Furnace of Affliction

"Look, I have refined you, but not as silver; I
have tested you in the furnace of affliction."
ISAIAH 48:10

Years ago, the furnace of affliction burned hotter than normal. My life became a waking nightmare as a single parent
with a failing body, living with adolescent daughters who carried
their own intense pain. I knew no one could fix this for me.

God refined me through that white-hot fire and drew me
to Him in ways nothing else ever has, but living in the furnace
wasn't easy. This is my present-tense account of how it can feel:

As the heat intensifies, I feel like I can't go on. I wonder how
I can endure with grace when the heat is almost smothering me
and I'm struggling to breathe. It's moment to moment. Breath by
breath. I can't think about the future in the furnace. All I can do
is pray I'll survive, as I wonder if God will ever deliver me.

When I get up in the morning, the air is already thick as my
thoughts run to what the day might hold. I force myself to pull

out my Bible and start talking to God, begging Him to lower the temperature. I tell Him my fears and anxious thoughts, as I pore over Scripture, looking for something, anything, to cling to.

When I do that, strangely I can breathe normally. It's as if I've walked out of the furnace for a few minutes and the heaviness is gone. I feel hopeful, almost weightless, as everything but God fades into the background. He shows me things I've never seen, and I start underlining in my Bible everywhere, aware that God is speaking to me. Sometimes I sit and listen, taking in the holiness of the moment, and other times I'm racing to record all that God is saying. Scripture now brims with promises and hope as passages I've hurriedly skimmed before take on new meaning. Now I linger over them. Savor their sweetness. They are as honey in my mouth, and I know they will sustain me throughout the day.

Though my regular life feels dark, here the light breaks through the clouds. I feel alive here and long to stay in this place forever, beholding the beauty of the Lord. I'm unearthing treasures I can't find elsewhere, echoing the words of Samuel Rutherford, who said, "I rejoice that he is come and has chosen [me] in the furnace"[31] as He whispers that I am His.

Our experience in the furnace can transform us, as God opens our eyes to His gifts in the fire. The heat brings a deeper portion of Christ and a deeper delight in His Word. We learn to cling to God alone and not anything He gives us. While the furnace of affliction can be unspeakably hot, through it God is refining us, turning our pain into tested silver and gold that will last throughout eternity.

REFLECT: When have you felt the greatest heat in the furnace of affliction? And what brought you relief in those desperate days?

The Agony of Waiting

[Abraham] did not waver in unbelief at God's
promise but was strengthened in his faith and gave
glory to God, because he was fully convinced that
what God had promised, he was also able to do.

ROMANS 4:20–21

Waiting can be agonizing.

It's hardest to wait when I'm uncertain about the outcome. When I'm trusting God for the best while preparing for the worst. It would be much easier if I had a guaranteed good outcome or some reassurance to anchor my prayers. But God often seems silent when I'm waiting. I have no idea whether He'll ever answer my prayer, so I feel like I'm waiting in the dark.

I have read and reread Psalm 13:1: "How long, O LORD? Will you forget me forever?" (ESV). I have asked that question many times. Any answer, even a no, would feel easier than "Wait."

Several years ago, I searched the Bible to find a promise that would help me during a torturous wait. When I read the verse, I was frustrated. While I admired Abraham's faith, I could see why he didn't waver. He had a direct word from God. I wanted God to give me a promise like that, so I kept begging Him for a sign.

None came. In the end God's answer was no.

At first I struggled to make sense of those seemingly wasted years. While I had grown closer to God, I wondered why God hadn't answered me sooner.

Several years later, as I began reading Romans again, I hesitated at Romans 4. It painfully reminded me of that time of asking and waiting. Feeling disconnected from Abraham, I decided to look at his life in Genesis.

Studying Genesis, I saw that while Abraham was waiting, God was working. Molding his character. Teaching him patience. In that twenty-five-year wait Abraham got to know God intimately. In those seemingly wasted years, God transformed him. I saw Abraham's impatience in the process. He too had tried to help God fulfill his plans.

I thought Abraham's faith was in God's promise of descendants, but if it was, he wouldn't have been willing to sacrifice Isaac, the son he'd waited decades for. I realized then that Abraham's faith was rooted in the Promiser. He wasn't holding on to a particular outcome; he was holding on to God.

You and I have the same assurance Abraham did—that God will provide everything we need. If you let that promise sink in, you may see your waiting differently. Perhaps God is making me, and you, wait for the same reasons He made Abraham wait. To make us attentive to His voice. To deepen our relationship. To solidify our trust.

In retrospect, I can see that "Wait" is the most precious answer God can give us. It makes us cling to Him rather than cling to an outcome. God knows what we need. We do not. He sees the future. We cannot. His perspective is eternal. Ours is not. He will give us what is best for us. *When* it is best for us.

WRITE: Spend a few minutes writing about something you've been waiting for. Notice and record the ways God has provided everything you need in the meantime. How have you become more attentive to God's voice in the wait? How has your relationship with Him deepened? How has your wait changed you?

61

Trusting God
in the Painful Present

None of the good promises the LORD had made to
the house of Israel failed. Everything was fulfilled.

JOSHUA 21:45

L ooking back on suffering is so different from the immediate
experience of walking through it." A friend just texted me
those words, and they are just what I needed today. I know one
day I will see God's hand in my life, but now, in the midst of it,
I have little objectivity. I don't have eloquent reflections on what
I'm learning. I'm simply living.

Right now, I'm not just talking about God's presence; I'm
experiencing it. With a difficult future in front of me, I feel
a sense of peace knowing God will walk me through it that I
couldn't have felt thirty years ago. Back then, I hadn't experienced God's faithfulness and didn't know that God would fulfill
all His promises. I was far more anxious than trusting.

WATCHING FOR THE MORNING

I think of Joseph's story in Genesis. He was betrayed by his brothers and sold as a slave in Egypt. After he rose to a position of trust in Potiphar's house, his master's wife falsely accused him of attempted rape, and Joseph was thrown into prison, where he remained for years. Joseph had no idea how his story would end. While God later delivered Joseph in an astonishing way, the beauty of Joseph's story is not in the miraculous deliverance but in God's constant and faithful care.

I remember years of crying out to God, thinking my faith would get back on track when life got back to normal. But as the pain grew more intense, I realized I needed to find God in the present and not wait for my circumstances to improve. God wanted me to find Him sufficient in the midst of trouble rather than just demanding that He deliver me from it.

But now I know—from studying Scripture, from knowing God more deeply, from lived experience and not just academic knowledge—anything the Lord brings into my life will ultimately be for my good. Even when it doesn't feel good right now. And I don't know if it ever will. In fact, I don't know how much pain that "good" will entail. The road may be harder than I expect (even writing those words makes me cringe), yet I know He will pour out His grace when I need it. Nonetheless, the suffering will still be painful.

The physical aspects of suffering are no different for those who trust the Lord than for those who don't know Him, meaning our pain is just as painful, but what's different is our hope. Those who trust God have an unfading hope. We know God has good plans for us, that He will never leave us, and that He will keep His promises. We can attest, like Joshua, that none of God's promises have failed. And they never will. We who have a history of seeing God's faithfulness know that our hope is sure. Even if right now, today, we must hold onto those words by faith.

REFLECT: Over the years, how have you been tempted to believe that your faith will get back on track when your circumstances change? In contrast, how will you seek God in the present, rather than waiting for your circumstances to improve?

62

God Knows What I Need

The LORD is my shepherd;
I have what I need.
PSALM 23:1

I already have everything I need. Scripture tells me that, and I want to believe it, but it doesn't feel true. There are things I want, that I long for, that I think I need, and yet I don't have them. So accepting that I have what I need is a truth I need to lean into as much as it is a promise I can hold on to. If I don't have it, and God hasn't supplied it, then I don't need it.

A dear friend of mine has a young daughter who wakes up every night with deep brain seizures that leave her shaking. It's a life-threatening condition, so my friend is always on guard, never fully asleep, watching her little daughter, praying the seizure will stop quickly. When we were recently talking, she said, "I feel my greatest need is just to sleep, but I know from Scripture if I really needed it, God would provide it. And so I'm trusting that."

I kept thinking about her words, asking God to show me too that if I don't have something, I really don't need it. Her attitude reminds me of John Newton's words: "All shall work together for good; everything is needful that He sends; nothing can be needful that He withholds."[32]

This outlook can help us trust God when we are not getting what we've been praying for. We don't need to frantically run around, assuming God isn't watching over us, or that God won't take care of us, or that what we are praying for is essential for us. If it were necessary, God would provide it.

The hymn "Great Is Thy Faithfulness" is a beautiful reminder for me. The hymn writer looks back and sees that he lacked nothing he needed. God was faithful through everything. But notice the words are in the past tense: "All I have needed, Thy hand hath provided. Great is thy faithfulness, Lord, unto me!"[33] It's easier to see God's hand in the events of the past, the ways He's carried us, how He turned what we thought was devastating into a blessing. But when we look to the future, we often doubt His care and provision, convinced we know what's best for us.

We can be assured God is doing today's work on our prayer and will always give us what we need. Matthew Henry wrote about Psalm 23:1: "I shall be supplied with whatever I need; and if I have not everything I desire, I may conclude it is either not fit for me, or not good for me, or I shall have it in due time."[34]

God is in charge of your life and tenderly cares for you. He laid down His life for you. Since He holds the universe and can change your situation in a word, you can be sure He will give you everything you need.

We can all repeat with David, "The Lord is my shepherd; I have what I need."

MEMORIZE: Write today's verse on an index card. Put it where you'll see it regularly so you can memorize it.

Bad Theology Blames the Sufferer

*"For as heaven is higher than earth, so
my ways are higher than your ways, and
my thoughts than your thoughts."*

ISAIAH 55:9

Years ago, contrary to dire weather forecasts, a hurricane missed our area, but much of the surrounding area was devastated by the storm. My friend and I were thankful we were spared, but her explanation surfaced deeper questions. She said, "I know why we were spared catastrophe, and the storm circled our town and went south. I was praying that God would keep us safe, and He answered my prayers!"

God does answer our prayers, but I wondered: *Why does God miraculously heal some people and not others? Why does disaster strike one city and not another? Can we simply draw straight lines between our requests and God's answers?*

I once heard a pastor tell of his cancer that went into remission. When he told his congregation, several said, "We knew God would heal you because so many people were praying for you." While the pastor was thankful for others' prayers, he also knew that faithful believers throughout the ages have earnestly prayed and yet not been healed. The apostle Paul was not healed in order that God might show that His power could be made perfect in Paul's weakness (2 Cor. 12:8–9).

In Acts 12, James was killed while Peter was rescued, and I wondered why God let James die and Peter live. Did James not have enough faith? Or were people not praying for James?

From Scripture we know God's ways are not our ways (Isa. 55:8). Living or dying, being spared or being tortured, being delivered in this life or the next is not an indicator of God's love for us or the measure of our faith. Nothing can separate us from God's love (Rom. 8:35), and our future is determined by what He knows is best for us.

Still, prosperity gospel proponents have told me that if I had prayed in faith, my body would have been healed, my son would have been spared, and my marriage would have been restored. It was all up to me. Their words have left me bruised and disillusioned, but that understanding of God is not the gospel. God's response to our prayers is not dependent on our worthiness but rather rests on His great mercy.

If you are in Christ, God is completely for you. Your struggles are not because you didn't pray the right way or because you didn't pray enough or because you have weak faith or insufficient intercessors. It is because God is using your suffering in ways you may not understand now, but one day you will. One day you will see how God used your affliction to prepare you for an incomparable weight of glory. This is the gospel. And it holds for all who love Christ.

––––––––––––––––

REFLECT: How have you been negatively impacted by a prosperity gospel that insists you are responsible for the suffering you endure? What do you need to remind yourself of to counter the lies of that false teaching?

Praying for Only
One Outcome

Trust in the LORD with all your heart, and
do not rely on your own understanding.

PROVERBS 3:5

God's ways are not my ways. And so He often calls me to die to my need to understand. Too often, I rely on my research, my instincts, my understanding of God, more than I trust in Him.

I want to understand everything, especially when I'm suffering. I want to know why. Yet God's ways are higher than mine, beyond my knowing, often shrouded in mystery. I simply need to trust Him as I release my hold on the outcome I've been clinging to.

Years ago, I was begging God to bring my husband back to our family. He was living with another woman, but I knew God could change his heart. I was asking God to grant him repentance, which I assumed would result in him joyfully returning, begging for forgiveness, and winning us all back.

After all, we were Christians and held marriage as sacred. Yet months turned into years, and I was still banging on God's door, pleading daily for a miracle; I couldn't imagine God would want any other outcome. In my mind, my husband's return would display the gospel most brightly. It would help our daughters see the beauty of faith. It would repair what Satan had broken. So there was no way to pray for anything else.

Then one day as I was talking to my counselor about my prayers, she said, "You've prayed for years for this to happen. Trust that God is hearing you. But perhaps you may need to stop setting your heart on just one outcome."

I was shocked by her words. I felt like I'd be giving up. Weren't we supposed to keep asking and believing in prayer? How could God want a different outcome than this one? If we ultimately couldn't restore our marriage, why would God let me pray for years with hope?

I saw that in praying for God's will to be done, I needed to slowly open my hand and release the outcome I was clutching. I realized my hope wasn't in an outcome; my hope was in God, regardless of the outcome. I wasn't clinging to what I thought was best, I was clinging to God, who knew what was best.

In the end, I didn't get the outcome I had been praying for, but God had much more in store for me. He was leading me somewhere new, somewhere deeper, somewhere wonderful, but the path was steep and rocky. I had to let Him lead the way and hold tightly onto me.

PRAY: Lord, I confess that *my way* out of the suffering in which I'm stuck is the only way that seems right. Show me the outcomes I've been clinging to so I can release them to You. Teach me how to trust You with all my heart and lean not on my own understanding.

Can I Find Peace in Pain?

You will keep the mind that is dependent on
you in perfect peace, for it is trusting in you.
ISAIAH 26:3

Opening my scrapbook, I was flooded with emotion. Katie's preschool card said: "What's your mom's favorite hobby?" Her answer: "Making meals for people."

My throat tightened. I was no longer that person. I once loved to cook for people.

But why was I crying? I'd been dealing with this weakness for years. When the tears wouldn't stop, I prayed, "Show me what to do. I want peace," and the words "In acceptance lies peace" came to mind. The four words are from a poem by Amy Carmichael titled "In Acceptance Lieth Peace," which she wrote after a broken leg left her bedridden and in great pain for the rest of her life. In the poem, Carmichael detailed the futile ways we often deal with loss.[35]

The first way is to avoid reminders of the past, trying to forget the hurt. The second is to stay busy so there's no time to think. The third is to deny it and pretend there never was any pain. The fourth is to resign ourselves to a life of unceasing misery. The fifth approach is to accept this new way of living, knowing that God will go through it with us.

Though the first four options sound depressing, I've tried them all. Maybe you have as well. They promised relief but left me numb. Acceptance is different. It stops turmoil and leads to peace. Elisabeth Elliot would agree. In a letter to her parents after her husband's murder, she wrote, "I can only say that the peace I have literally passes all understanding. I have learned the lesson Amy Carmichael speaks of in her poem: 'In acceptance lieth peace.' I accept, gratefully, from the hand of God, this experience."[36]

Gratefully accepting everything from God, including your husband's murder, makes no sense apart from Christ. Yet by faith, she was able to experience God's peace in tragedy. Fifty years later she wrote, "God included the hardships of my life in His original plan. Nothing takes Him by surprise. His plan is to make me holy. All I have to do is accept it."[37]

All I have to do is accept it. It sounds simple, but you may have realized, as I have, that it is not easy. To do that we need to believe that God has a purpose in our pain. And that He is with us in it.

Thumbing through the scrapbook again, I remember that the Lord will one day transform my suffering into eternal joy. If He has allowed something into my life, it is the best thing for me. One day in heaven we will see how everything God brought into my life was out of love.

PRACTICE: Take a deep breath and know that God is with you in this moment. Reflecting on a significant loss in your life, say these words aloud: "I trust Your love and Your provision. So I can say, 'In acceptance lies peace.'" Then, be still with God.

Do You Wish You Had Accomplished More?

When I considered all that I had accomplished
and what I had labored to achieve, I found
everything to be futile and a pursuit of the wind.
There was nothing to be gained under the sun.
ECCLESIASTES 2:11

D o you ever wish you'd accomplished more? I do. But when
I'm discouraged, I look at John the Baptist's example. His
life began with great promise. An angelic proclamation. A call
from God. A thriving ministry. Yet it ended in obscurity—alone
in a small prison cell.

We celebrate people who begin with nothing and finish with
great accomplishments. We want to be remembered for something noteworthy, but when we haven't accomplished what we'd
hoped to, we may question what good our lives have been.

I started off wanting it all, which was at first a successful
career. After I got married and had children, I left my job and

spent all my energy on raising a family. So, when my husband filed for divorce and my daughters rebelled, I felt like a failure.

Mother Teresa's simple statement encouraged me then, and I've gone back to it throughout my life: "God did not call me to be successful. He called me to be faithful."[38]

John the Baptist would have agreed. Crowds flocked to him, and his ministry exploded before he was thirty. He baptized Jesus and might have assumed that he would minister at His side. But John was imprisoned a few months after Jesus began His public ministry. John's ministry evaporated and he died a humiliating death. From a worldly perspective, John looked like a failure.

Yet John was wildly successful in God's eyes. He had served a crucial purpose in the kingdom, faithfully preparing the way for Christ. He didn't see the full fruit of his ministry. Many of us never do.

Like me, do you wonder if there is anything noteworthy about your life? As Douglas McKelvey asked, "How many times have I felt then the gradually settling weight of disillusionment, of disappointment and confusion, when no great thing materialized, when no life-changing opportunity suddenly arrived at my doorstep, when no such moment of call or clarity was ever manifest at all?"[39]

Then McKelvey wisely reflected, "If you would pray to do great things for your God, then you must pray such prayers without regard for how they should be answered. . . . For it is not you that will do any great thing for God, but God laboring in you and through you will greatly accomplish his own good purposes according to the workings of his sovereignty and love.

Be liberated now from this burden of believing that anything depends upon you."[40]

As we continue to wrestle with these issues in our lives, I'm thankful that what we accomplish does not depend on us. It's not about our glory or our reputation or our success. God is the one who works in us and through us, and He who began a good work in us will be faithful to complete it (see Phil. 1:6).

WRITE: At the top of a page, write Mother Teresa's statement: "God did not call me to be successful. He called me to be faithful." Then make two columns: in the left column, list the ways you have strived to be successful; in the right column, list the ways God is calling you to be faithful.

67

Dependence Is Grace

You provided bread from heaven for their hunger;
you brought them water from the rock for their thirst.
NEHEMIAH 9:15

Surviving a crisis is more than making it through the first day of disaster, which is often a blur. It's like being thrown into the wilderness. We don't know how to survive, so we call out to God, and He strengthens us.

This is utter dependence on God. Somehow we are enduring because God is sustaining us. Whether we're kneeling or prostrate or in the fetal position, we recognize our helplessness before God. Moment by moment, we see our need for Him.

After my son Paul died, I felt God carrying me, but I spiraled downward months later. The God who once felt breathtakingly near now felt miles away.

This stage of unsettledness has occurred after every major crisis I've been through. I want to get out of the wilderness, to move past the pain, but I can't figure out how to escape.

Ted Wueste offers an invaluable perspective: "God doesn't leave us to fend for ourselves. We may feel alone but we aren't. He is leading us somewhere. The journey is about deepening our dependence on him. Why? Because dependence is the promised land. A life of dependence is the truest, most real hope in our lives. Our hope is in him, not some location outside of difficulty."[41]

This celebration of dependence may seem startling to you. It was to me. I often long for certainty more than I long for God. Yet as new suffering emerges, I'm learning to depend on God more closely. I realize that though the future feels uncertain to me, it is fully known to Him. Rather than feeling deserted by God in the wilderness, I can feel His presence more closely. I see how He is providing for me.

If you feel deserted in the wilderness right now, perhaps start by looking for signs of God's love that you may have overlooked, connecting the good things that have happened to you with God's love. Maybe God was loving you when you asked for peace, and it washed over you. He was loving you when you felt depressed, and a friend called unexpectedly. He was loving you when you opened the Bible, and a passage came alive. God may be showing you His love in countless ways—you may just need to pay attention.

If you're discouraged in the desert, desperate to escape, know that saints before you have felt that way. God provided for their daily needs, and He'll provide for yours as well. Trust that He is doing a deep work in your life, and ask Him to show you His presence and provision. Perhaps you'll discover that dependence truly is the promised land and that a life of dependence is a life of unending grace.

———————

REFLECT: What are the ways you've tried to escape depending on God alone? What would it look like to depend on God's unending grace? Where have you seen signs of God's love recently?

68

Finding Hope in Depression

Why, my soul, are you so dejected?
Why are you in such turmoil?
Put your hope in God, for I will still
praise him, my Savior and my God.

PSALM 43:5

Some days life feels relentless. My physical losses confront me daily, and I get tired of continually adjusting to a new normal. I want the old one back.

I feel myself slipping into depression, not knowing how to pull out. And this depression, which is largely based on the lies I'm telling myself, is much harder than the suffering itself.

God feels distant, mostly because I've been pulling away. But Psalm 43:2 pulls me back. Like the psalmist, I cry out, "For you are the God of my refuge. Why have you rejected me?"

For the psalmist, life was closing in and darkness was falling. He knew the Lord intimately, but he began to feel rejected.

But instead of listening to himself and spiraling downward, he started talking to God, asking, "Send your light and your truth; let them lead me" (v. 3). He knew God could lead him out of his own darkness and lies. After the psalmist talked to God and asked for help, he began talking to himself. He questioned why he was depressed, asking, "Why, my soul, are you so dejected? Why are you in such turmoil?" (v. 5).

I often feel vaguely depressed, unable to articulate the core of my fears. A particular unspoken lie that haunts me is, "It's only going to get worse; your life is going to be miserable." But when I write down what is troubling me, what is causing my turmoil, I can look at my situation biblically. Often voicing my fears gives me clarity and a fresh perspective. And if I'm able to follow my fears to the worst potential conclusion, I can see that God will be with me even then.

Finally, the psalmist told himself, "Put your hope in God, for I will still praise him, my Savior and my God" (v. 5). When everything still looked dark, the psalmist chose to tell himself the truth, based on who God is, rather than listen to himself, based on his own fears.

David Martyn Lloyd-Jones says, "Have you realized that most of your unhappiness in life is due to the fact that you are listening to yourself instead of talking to yourself?"[42]

When we listen to ourselves, the voices of self-pity and defeat become deafeningly loud. In those moments, God calls us to preach to ourselves by praying and reading the Bible. And repeating back to Him words of Scripture like these.

So today, when life feels overwhelming, will you recite God's promises and trust His words to you?

———————————

MEMORIZE: Write today's verse on an index card. Put it where you'll see it regularly so you can memorize it.

Weeping with Those Who Weep

How long, LORD? Will you forget me forever?
How long will you hide your face from me?

PSALM 13:1

How do you comfort your friends in a crisis? Do you sympathize with them, weep with them, and let them vent about how awful things are? Or do you tell them to trust God, remind them of His faithfulness, give them Scripture to hold onto? Most of us have a tendency to land on one side or the other. It's hard to do both in the same conversation.

For years I struggled with how to comfort people until I discovered the gift of lament. Praying a lament brings our loved ones before the Lord, as the friends did who lowered the paralytic to Jesus, trusting He can and will heal however He chooses. It is an invitation and opportunity to pour out our pain while renewing our confidence in the Lord.

When my friend Jeanne was diagnosed with ALS, the women in our small group went to pray with her regularly. As her body grew more frail, we were often at a loss for words and once simply prayed through Psalm 142, corporately lamenting together. We read a few verses and then, following the psalmist, added our own words of complaint and protest, moving to requests and pleas and ending in trust.

Lament allowed us to simultaneously acknowledge the terrors of ALS and all it would entail, crying and crying out for all that felt wrong, while trusting God together. Previously, we'd camped out on one extreme or the other, reinforcing that her situation was awful or reciting God's promises while ignoring her pain.

Psalm 13 is a great psalm to use for lament, both individually and with others. Mark Vroegop offers an insightful explanation of how to pray using this psalm:[43]

> **Turn to God.** Talk to God directly about what's happening (v. 1).
>
> **Bring your complaint.** Identify the pain you're facing and the questions you have in it (v. 2).
>
> **Ask boldly for help.** Seek God's help while you're in pain. Ask God for what you want (vv. 3–4).
>
> **Choose to trust.** Voice your trust, rehearse God's promises, remember His character (vv. 5–6).

When you have friends in crisis, I encourage you to use this psalm or another lament passage to support and pray with them. The psalms, which are the prayer book of the church, offer God's comfort rather than the platitudes we can be quick to offer. When we pray a lament psalm, we give our raw words of complaint and sometimes horror, weeping with those who weep, acknowledging the depths of our friends' pain. And after we have mourned with them, we collectively end with the truth of God's Word. We trust God together, rehearsing the truths we know both from Scripture and from experience. We remember God's goodness and faithfulness as we hold onto hope with our friends.

PRACTICE: Pray a prayer of lament using the pattern of Psalm 13: (1) turn to God; (2) bring your complain; (3) ask boldly for help; and (4) choose to trust God.

70

The Fruit of the Wilderness

"God has made me fruitful in the
land of my affliction."
GENESIS 41:52

What's the point of the wilderness anyway? I've asked that question numerous times when I've been lost in the desert, wondering if I'd ever find a way out. People told me that God was working, but since I didn't know what He was doing, I secretly wondered if He was doing anything at all.

I didn't choose the wilderness. No one does. It's a dark place of loneliness, rejection, and despair. But the wilderness also cultivates the most life-giving fruit because God shapes and molds us there, teaching us to trust Him alone.

Joseph named his second son Ephraim, saying, "God has made me fruitful in the land of my affliction." Joseph became fruitful in Egypt—the land where he was sold as a slave, where he was falsely accused, where he was imprisoned and seemingly forgotten. These were the ugliest, leanest years of Joseph's life, yet they may paradoxically have been the most beautiful because they taught Joseph to trust God.

I understand the beauty of Ephraim myself. The most difficult places in my life have produced the greatest fruit. Lilias Trotter, a missionary to Algeria in the late 1800s, said this: "Take the very hardest thing in your life—the place of difficulty, outward or inward, and expect God to triumph gloriously in that very spot. Just there he can bring your soul into blossom!"[44]

God triumphs in our place of struggle. The hardest things in our lives become the basis of our ministry. Our faith is often forged in the desert. But we can't produce fruit ourselves or bring our own souls into blossom. God produces life-giving fruit when we are attached to the vine, abiding in Christ. This happens naturally in the wilderness because we must depend on Him daily. We're starkly aware that apart from Him we can do nothing.

In the wilderness, I read the Bible more attentively than ever before and learned to love God for who He is and not for what He could do for me. Some people wander from faith in suffering, wondering if God even exists, but those who have met God in the fire, whose faith is forged in the wilderness, know that He is real.

If you are in the desert now, don't assume that because you haven't seen fruit yet, you won't see it. The most important fruit is of the Spirit, an inward dependence on God that radiates love, joy, and peace to others. As we look to God in our suffering, trusting Him for all we need, He will ensure that we are fruitful in the land of our affliction.

PRAY: Lord, I am lost in the wilderness, feeling lonely, rejected, and desperate. Please help me sense that You're with me in this barren place of struggle. Build in me the kind of sturdy faith that can only be forged in the wilderness. Teach me to depend completely on You, Lord, so that I can radiate Your love, joy, and peace to others.

71

What Truths Do We Cling to in Suffering?

*What no eye has seen, no ear has heard, and
no human heart has conceived—God has
prepared these things for those who love him.*

1 CORINTHIANS 2:9

When a close friend was diagnosed with a terminal disease, I was shaken. I, who write about suffering, had no words to offer. Words seemed inadequate. Trite. Even condescending. How do you encourage someone who is beginning a devastating journey into the unknown?

It took me days to process what was happening. Our friends were struggling to process it too. As we prayed, we tried to remind ourselves of the truths we knew. Bedrock truths that carried us through our own grief. Truths that every Christian can hold onto. Truths that will bear the weight of our sorrow.

First and foremost, God is sovereign. Nothing that happens to us is a surprise to Him. Not one sparrow falls to the ground apart from the Father's will (Matt. 10:29). The God of the universe, who keeps the earth spinning on its axis, who tells the ocean to come this far and no farther (Job 38:11), who commands the wind and the waves (Mark 4:41), who clothes the lilies of the field (Matt. 6:28–30), and who has numbered the hairs on our head (Luke 12:7), can ensure that all things work together for good for those who love Him (Rom. 8:28).

God has numbered our days. All our days were determined by God before we even took our first breath (Ps. 139:16). Nothing can cut short our lives. No one will live one second less than God determined before the foundation of the world.

God walks with us every minute of our lives. He will always be with us, to the end of the age (Matt. 28:20). We will never drink a bitter cup, walk through a dark valley, or endure any pain without Him. He will never leave us.

Christ will give us the comfort and strength we need each day. He will never forsake us, especially in our darkest hour. We don't need to understand how we will face the future because God will give us all we need every day that we have breath. As Deuteronomy 33:25 assures us, "As your days, so shall your strength be" (ESV).

One day our eyes will close in death and open to the breathtaking reality that we are in the presence of our Savior. We will feel more alive, more vibrant, more energetic, and more joyful than we ever have on earth. The God whom we have known but never seen will be before us. We will behold His glory with our own eyes, with no distortion or filter. Our souls will be completely at rest and at peace, filled to the measure of all the fullness of God. We can't yet comprehend all God has awaiting us, but we know it will be glorious.

These are the truths we as Christians base our lives on. They are sure and unchanging promises, guaranteed by the One who holds the universe. No matter what happens, we will never walk alone.

PRACTICE: What truths do you need to cling to in your current situation? And is there a truth from today you want to encourage someone else with? Look up one of the verses and write it down to remind yourself.

Embrace the Life You Have

"Remember not the former things, nor consider the things of old. Behold, I am doing a new thing; now it springs forth, do you not perceive it? I will make a way in the wilderness and rivers in the desert."

ISAIAH 43:18–19 ESV

I still buy art supplies. Or at least, I put them in my online shopping cart. I imagine myself creating a masterpiece or just doodling on scrap paper, and I forget that my hands don't function as they once did.

While I am convinced I'm living out God's best for me, there are days I mourn what used to be—particularly as I go through old boxes, each one filled with memories of a life that no longer exists. Especially the crates of art supplies. Twenty years ago, my life was defined by projects I could do with my hands. Painting, crafting, scrapbooking. They all sparked my creativity and made me happy.

But my diagnosis of post-polio syndrome changed all that. The doctors told me that the more I do, the weaker I'll get, so I can't do anything frivolous with my energy. With my arms deteriorating, I couldn't afford to waste my energy on crafts. I boxed everything up (with help) and shoved it into the attic.

As a friend helped me rummage through those old boxes, I decided to give those supplies away so someone else could enjoy them. Yet a deep sadness settled over me. I miss those things. I know they are part of my past, and I can't dwell on what can't be undone, but it's still hard.

This grieving isn't particular to me. You've faced disappointments. Your life may look different than you imagined it would.

So, what should we do? How do we get past the disappointment of losing a precious part of our life? We can pretend we don't miss it, or we can lean in and acknowledge what's hard.

Only when we recognize the longing can we give it to God. When we verbalize it, and what it's attached to, the sadness loses some of its grip. The things we love will always be a part of us, but their loss doesn't have to devastate us or define us.

This counsel from John Piper has been immeasurably helpful: "Occasionally weep deeply over the life you hoped would be. Grieve the losses. Then wash your face. Trust God. And embrace the life you have."[45]

Embracing means gladly receiving and even welcoming whatever the Lord gives me, even when it wasn't in my plans. It means being fully present, living in the now, finding joy in the moment, and not constantly longing for what was in the past.

Into a world of sadness and loss, God told His people not to remember the past because He was making a new way in the wilderness. While we may always remember what we've lost, we can be sure God is making a way in the wilderness and rivers in the desert. Lean into His work and embrace it. Trust that God is doing something beautiful.

WRITE: Spend time writing about a loss or disappointment you've endured. Name every detail, consequence, and grief of the situation. Include all your emotions, even the ones you'd rather forget. Then take a deep breath and sit with God for a few minutes without writing. When you're ready, tell God you're willing to receive the new thing He is doing in you.

73

What Desolation Looks Like

My God, my God, why have you abandoned me?
Why are you so far from my deliverance
and from my words of groaning?
PSALM 22:1

As I've struggled to make sense of feeling desolate, I've held onto the image of Holy Saturday. Holy Saturday is the long day of waiting and feeling abandoned after the horror of Good Friday.

Good Friday was the death of the disciples' dreams and what once felt certain. They would have been devastated as Jesus was crucified, unable to figure out why and what was happening. I've been through days that felt like Good Friday when the unthinkable happened and I lived through my worst fears.

Holy Saturday follows Good Friday, which for the disciples was Sabbath, a day without work. Nothing to do but reflect on the terror of what they'd witnessed. Did they wonder what was real about what they'd earnestly believed days earlier?

Holy Saturday follows our own catastrophic losses. The day we realize our dreams have been crushed and we're not sure how to move forward—or if we even want to. Long days or even years of waiting in limbo, trying to process what has happened. We wonder if we dare voice our disappointment with God. We ask, "Has He abandoned us?" as we wonder what was real about our faith.

It's important on Holy Saturday to acknowledge all we've lost as we face our doubts and disappointments. We may want to rush past this day, to "fix" others who are waiting in it, to offer trite answers to ease the pain. But rather than platitudes or quick solutions, we need to sit with the questions.

Holy Saturday doesn't have the fury and flurry of Good Friday, but it's still tense. And intense. I've had friends walk away from faith as they wonder why God didn't rescue them. Why did He let them hope and make plans, only to have them crumble? Disillusioned, they assumed that if God exists, He's forsaken them.

If they, and you, could only hear the whispers of God's voice, hear the song He's singing over you, hear the tears He's weeping with you, then you might view it differently. But you may hear nothing. Just silence. Yet if you can stay and keep looking at Jesus, you'll experience God's love as the disciple John did. John stayed to the end, watching from the foot of the cross, and became as firmly convinced of God's love as anyone who's ever lived. His identity was as one beloved. When you've been through the worst and found God faithful, Christ's love will be as firmly nailed to your identity as His body was nailed to the cross.

For all of us who've watched our nightmares come true and cried bitter tears in the dark, we can be sure the story isn't over yet. As Jesus promises, "I will not leave you desolate; I will come to you" (John 14:18 RSV). So, if you are living in the agonizing intensity of Holy Saturday, can you hang on a bit longer knowing Easter is coming?

REFLECT: What are your doubts and disappointments? Be honest. After you've acknowledged them, ask God to give you the strength to hang on, knowing that Easter is coming.

74

Keeping Your Eyes on the Lord

"We do not know what to do,
but our eyes are on you."
2 CHRONICLES 20:12 ESV

When Katie was learning to drive, her instructor constantly reminded the students to keep their eyes on the road. To keep them fixed on a point straight ahead without being distracted. Otherwise, the car would be headed in whatever direction they were looking. The instructor smiled and added, "If you notice a cute guy on the sidewalk and keep looking at him, you'll be headed right for him!"

Given my driving skills, I needed that lesson more than Katie did. At sixteen, I ran over a friend's mailbox with my car as I was admiring her azalea bushes, and then seconds later I took out the aforementioned shrubbery as well.

Katie's instructor's words have stayed with me, not only for driving but for life. We're headed toward whatever we're looking at. Given that, I want to keep my eyes on Jesus and not on what is happening around me.

King Jehoshaphat kept his eyes on the Lord in the midst of a crisis in 2 Chronicles 20. A huge army was coming toward him, and he was completely unprepared. He said to the Lord, "We are powerless against this great horde that is coming against us. We do not know what to do, but our eyes are on you" (2 Chron. 20:12 ESV). This verse has become my go-to cry to the Lord when I'm overwhelmed.

When we keep our eyes on Jesus, we know we can trust Him. As Peter did, when Jesus bid him to come to Him on the water. When Peter was focused on the Lord, looking straight ahead, he could easily walk on the water. But as soon as Peter looked away, distracted by the wind and waves, he began to sink.

If your eyes are on Jesus, you can be unafraid regardless of how impossible the circumstances may seem. You can be confident God will take care of you. He who calmed the sea and gave sight to the blind can do anything. He can fix your problems in ways you could not even imagine.

Yet the minute you look away, you may get overwhelmed or fall into despair. If the storm continues, you may become a "quiet quitter," not overtly walking away but passively disengaging from the Lord. Going through the motions of faith while focusing on everything but Him. Feverishly researching, trusting in your own abilities rather than God, leaving you anxious and desperate. I have fallen into that trap in my own life.

Yet when I turn back to Jesus, I realize I don't need to solve my problems by myself, assuming it's all up to me. We can trust

God as we hold onto Him rather than clutching the outcome we want. He may do what seems impossible, allowing us to walk on water like Peter or be victorious against the odds like Jehoshaphat. But regardless of what happens, when we fix our eyes on Jesus, we can always find peace in the storm.

———————

MEMORIZE: Write today's verse on an index card. Put it where you'll see it regularly so you can memorize it.

75

When We Can't Imagine Living Like This

"Give us this day our daily bread."
MATTHEW 6:11 ESV

I vividly remember when my arms completely stopped working. I couldn't even button my shirt, and I knew the day would probably keep getting worse. As I struggled with every little thing, I wondered how I'd manage if I permanently lost use of my arms.

I cried out to the Lord, frustrated and scared, telling Him that this wasn't fair and that I wasn't prepared to deal with this now. I asked and then begged Him to fix it. Immediately. I ended by declaring, "I can't live like this for the rest of my life. I just can't do it!"

Then I was quiet. As I was trying to calm down, I heard the words, "I'm not asking you to live like this for the rest of your life. I'm just asking you to live like this today."

I knew that God was speaking to me and was immediately enveloped by peace. A supernatural unexpected peace that could only come from God. Nothing had changed in my circumstances, but everything looked different. Today was a finite period I could focus on. Today seemed doable. Today was much less frightening than the rest of my life. Coping with anything today seemed possible. Possible, that is, with God.

I remembered that Jesus taught us to ask for what we need each day, praying, "Give us today our daily bread." He will meet my needs today. His grace is available for today. God reminded me that my future was in His hands. Since His mercies are new every morning, tomorrow could bring miraculous joy and relief; I didn't need to despair over what would happen.

Yet God wasn't reassuring me that my circumstances would get better if I prayed the right prayer. No, He was asking for something that required a much deeper faith and trust. He was asking me to endure for today and trust Him for tomorrow.

He reassured me that through my weakness His strength would pour through me. He would supply all my needs—not in advance so I wouldn't need to rely on Him daily. But He would provide for me day by day, moment by moment, breath by breath.

We cannot imagine how God will provide in the future because we aren't there yet. Ed Welch says, "When you try to think about tomorrow without having yet received power for tomorrow, you will be anxious. . . . You do not yet have tomorrow's grace, so your imagination will tell an incomplete story of the future."[46]

My pain and strength ebb and flow daily, so I often don't know what to expect. But even when the day holds suffering, I know that God is not asking me to live with this pain and weakness for the rest of my life; He is just asking me to live with it today. I don't know what tomorrow will hold, but I know that regardless of what happens, God will provide all I need.

———————

REFLECT: In what struggle do you need God's grace to make it through today? In that struggle, what "daily bread" will you ask God to give you?

76

Is Our Hope Centered on Healing in This Life?

If in Christ we have hope in this life only,
we are of all people most to be pitied.
1 CORINTHIANS 15:19 ESV

I remember sitting through an indie play in my twenties when one of the characters turned to the audience and said, "None of us know when we're going to die. It could be you. Tonight."

Fear gripped me. I thought about her words all the way home, and that night I lay in bed terrified that I would die unexpectedly or be alone at my death. And I was a Christian.

Even now I don't think of death fondly. When I hear someone has a terminal illness, my prayers are centered on healing. I want God to give them more days. Death feels uncertain and painful, the end of all we know or understand. I don't want to die, and I don't want my loved ones to die either, even when they know Jesus. When they die, I will rejoice for them (though I will mourn their loss), but until they take their last breath, I want them to live.

I'm asking myself as I write this, Do we not see that for Christians, death is a passage from one life to the next? A passage from a world filled with sorrow and suffering, disappointments and disasters, to a world of unending joy. Suffering will disappear the minute we cross the threshold with Jesus into heaven. And yet we spend most of our energy not wanting that to happen. Do we see that heaven is what we are all longing for? That dying means someone has finished their work on earth, that they have run the race well, and that God has called them to enter the joy of their Master? Or do we conclude that their dying is a sign they didn't have the faith to be healed?

When Christians rail against death or assume people who are not healed didn't have enough faith, we look just like the world. People whose hope is in this life, who assume this life is better than heaven, who do whatever they can to stay here. But we know our hope is in so much more than this life, and endless joy awaits us in heaven.

Hezekiah in the Old Testament begged God to save his life on earth, but New Testament saints like Stephen willingly relinquished his life, looking to heaven. Apostles like Paul were certain it was far better to depart and be with Christ, saying, "For me, to live is Christ and to die is gain" (Phil. 1:21).

We'll miss our loved ones when they're gone, so it's a natural desire to want them to live longer. And since we're instinctively afraid of pain, it makes sense to want healing, both for ourselves and for those we love. But even as we do that, God calls us to remember that heaven holds a greater reward. So when the time comes, God will hold our hands and walk us into a world of unending glory and joy.

————————

PRAY: God, You know the ways I fear death for myself and those I love. Help me focus on You instead of my fears, knowing that believers don't need to fear death. For You are always with us, and heaven will be glorious.

77

What Are Your
Temptations in Suffering?

*"Stay awake and pray, so that you
won't enter into temptation."*
MATTHEW 26:41

I went to bed irritated last night and woke up equally annoyed.
Somehow no one could do anything right. People were asking
me to do things I didn't want to do. They were inconsiderate.
Unhelpful. Thoughtless.

With the frustrations of the previous day fresh in my mind,
I began detailing my sense of unsettledness. The more I thought
about it, the more convinced I was that no one was prioritizing
me. And then I read it. In the garden of Gethsemane, Jesus was
exhorting His disciples to pray for themselves, that they would
not enter into temptation in their suffering.

Jesus wasn't asking the disciples to pray for Him but rather
to pray about the temptations they would each soon be facing.
When I asked the Lord how this might apply to me, I realized

that my irritation was one way I succumb to sin in suffering. Of course, I don't see it as my sin in the moment. I think other people are sinning against me. I'm the wounded one.

When everyone is irritating me, the problem usually lies with me.

Jesus knew the disciples needed to spend time in prayer. Their worlds were about to be ripped apart, and they had no idea what was ahead. In their ignorance of their great need, they fell asleep despite Jesus's earnest request to stay awake. He knew they needed to be alert, to recognize what was happening, and to pray for themselves.

Temptations in suffering can be overwhelming, and each of us faces unique struggles. Do you know when you are most vulnerable? Are you on guard, watching for the signs? As we see later from the disciples, they were tempted to doubt. To deny what they knew to be true. To run away in panic and to lose hope. To let the reality of present pain overshadow all they had learned. To forget the truths Jesus spent years teaching them when their security was threatened.

I'm tempted to do all the above in suffering. When pain and loss are pressing in, I focus on my unmet needs and all that I wish was different. And if I don't recognize these as temptations from Satan, I will be convinced that I'm justified in my attitude. I won't see others' needs, their limitations, their attempts to help, or their internal struggles but will expect everyone to do what I want.

When I saw my sin this morning, I cried out to the Lord and asked Him to rescue me. To reorient my perspective and recognize that only He can meet my needs. To realize that I am called to love others rather than keeping an account of how well they've loved me.

This day and every day, I need His transforming grace.

———————

PRACTICE: Ask God to show you what your temptations are in suffering. As you sit with the Lord, write down the struggles that come to mind. Will you actively pray about those temptations the next time you are in distress?

78

Do the Next Thing

*I told them how the gracious hand of my
God had been on me . . . and their hands
were strengthened to do this good work.*

Nehemiah 2:18

Last year I faced multiple health crises, and I was often exhausted, struggling with crushing fatigue and discouragement. So many things had been left undone. My desk, piled with things to do, seemed too daunting even to approach. I didn't know where to start. Since I couldn't do everything, I wondered if I should bother to do anything.

When I felt overwhelmed, I remembered Elisabeth Elliot's advice. Advice that has taken me through numerous trials and countless days. Days when I felt inundated, and it seemed impossible to accomplish anything.

Do the next thing.

These four simple words have fueled me through the mundane and the monumental, and they have brought clarity and strength when I needed it.

These words gave me a framework after my son died. "Do the next thing" meant take a shower. Write the obituary. Plan a funeral. And afterwords, it was invaluable advice in grieving when I still had the daily tasks of life before me. Make dinner. Beg God for grace. Do the laundry. Read the Bible. Call a friend. Take a nap.

Then and even more recently, I just wanted to curl up in a ball and cry. Give in to self-pity. Make it all go away. But I know I can't escape indefinitely.

By just doing the next thing, I was able to make it through. I had enough light for the next step, and that was all I needed.

I had to do the next thing in the strength that God provided and trust He would supply the rest too. While the future looked dim and unknown, I knew everything was under His loving sovereign control. I had to take God's hand in the dark, trust He would guide my steps, and then act on the information in front of me. That lifted the weight of my decisions. I didn't need to figure it all out or understand everything. He would make my paths straight. I just needed to be connected to God. To hear His voice. To be still. And most of all, to trust Him.

When you feel overwhelmed at the enormity of a situation, begin by tackling the easiest task. And then move to the things you've been putting off because they are either unpleasant or you don't know where they'll lead. The projects you feel inadequate to fully face will be easier to handle one item at a time, seeing each step forward as a step toward God.

If you're feeling discouraged or overwhelmed, I encourage you just to do the next thing. Pray and trust God with the results. His yoke is easy, and His burden is light (see Matt. 11:30). He will guide you as you look to Him.

Just do the next thing.

————————

WRITE: Quiet your heart as you sit with God for a few minutes. Begin processing what you're facing now by writing down where you feel particularly stuck today. Then ask God to reveal what your next step should be. And then the next one. And then the next one.

Can God Use Our Broken Dreams?

"You planned evil against me; God planned it for good to bring about the present result—the survival of many people."

GENESIS 50:20

God is using this.

I say those words to myself all the time as a reminder that what's happening right now has a purpose beyond what I can see. That was the phrase I focused on one year, spelling it out in blocks so that I'd remember it. I wanted to keep reminding myself that God was using everything—from a broken vase to a broken body to broken dreams—for my good. Nothing would be wasted. Everything had a purpose. God's timing is always perfect.

Of course, we can see the beauty of God's timing only in retrospect. When we're in the middle, it just looks messy. We can't see the point of waiting. We're discouraged and wonder when, or even if, our suffering will end.

People in the Bible must have felt that way too. Joseph was likely bewildered after dropping from a favored son to a slave to a prisoner. Naomi assumed God was against her as she trekked home after the deaths of her husband and both of her sons. David may have wondered during Saul's murderous pursuit if God's promises to him would ever come true. We often read their stories with the underlying assumption that these men and women knew more than we do. That even when it looked hopeless, they knew God would turn it around.

We are all in the middle of the stories God is writing. Perhaps you've received a significant word from God, but it is interwoven with unspeakably hard circumstances that have left you screaming, "It's not supposed to be this way!" You may feel confused and bewildered, wondering what God is doing and how this could possibly end well.

Though you cannot see it now, you can trust that God is doing His deepest work right here, in your loneliness, in your disappointment, in your fear. Trust that there is purpose and movement happening that you cannot see, as you long for things to go back to the way they were. Your story is not over yet, and God is ordering every detail for His good and perfect plan. You are just waiting for it to unfold.

God is not delaying His deliverance for you. It will come at exactly the right moment. All that God has for you will be fulfilled at the appointed time. If it seems slow, if it feels messy, you just need to wait. It will surely come: it will not delay (see Hab. 2:3).

So, as you wait for what's coming, you can claim the greatest gift God has given you in trouble—His presence. God with us. We trust He is perfectly weaving together every pain, every sorrow, and every loss into a beautiful tapestry for His glory. And we can remind ourselves and one another, amid our broken dreams and changed plans, that God is using this.

REFLECT: Where has God taken what the enemy meant for evil and used it for good in your life? And where, today, are you still waiting to see God's goodness?

Letting God Speak in the Silence

"Speak, LORD, for your servant is listening."
I SAMUEL 3:9

I'm uncomfortable with silence. As a verbal processor, full of words, I try to fill even ten-second lulls in the conversation. Kristi recently informed me that after eight seconds of silence, I compulsively start talking. Even when I have nothing to say. She timed me to verify it. Children are so helpful, aren't they?

So you can understand why I avoided silent retreats. But when I finally attended one, I realized how much I needed quiet. In the silence I rediscovered myself. And God.

In the silence I could face the ugly things in my soul and the beauty of God's work in me. And in silence I could hear what was stirring inside me. The emotions I push aside because they make me cringe. The fears I suppress because I'd rather not face them. The sins I don't confess because I'd rather deny them. The longings I can't verbalize and dismiss as crazy dreams.

Everything that's buried deep inside of me comes out in silence. It's not neat and packaged. Just a jumble of thoughts and emotions. As these fragments bubble to the surface, I bring them to God and ask Him where they belong. Is He revealing something I need to see? Are these emotions to be dealt with or distractions to be pushed aside? Only He knows, and I offer them all to Him.

I often get frustrated that I'm not more focused. I want this time to be productive, yet what I gain in the silence is not measurable. Sometimes the Lord gives me direction and insight, but simply sitting with Jesus, listening for Him, waiting in His presence is what has transformed me.

Ted Wueste says in his book *Trusting God in the Wilderness*, "God desires so deeply for us to hear His tender voice . . . to listen to His heart more closely than the other voices that we believe will give us clarity . . . voices of the past, the voices of expectation, the voices of other people. . . . But God never stops speaking. He is always present and communicating."[47]

I wonder how much we miss because we're listening to the voices of the world, casually going about our days, unaware that God has so many things to tell us. God is constantly speaking to us, but are we listening?

We don't need silent retreats to hear God's voice. When we're intentionally listening, we can hear Him speaking throughout the day. For me it starts in the morning, as I light a candle and whisper, "Speak, Lord, your servant is listening."

MEMORIZE: Write today's verse on an index card. Put it where you'll see it regularly so you can memorize it.

How Suffering Ties Us to Christ

My goal is to know him and the power of his resurrection and the fellowship of his sufferings.

PHILIPPIANS 3:10

As my health deteriorates and each doctor's appointment seems to bring a more negative report, I shrink back at what might be coming. At the same time, I know that even if the worst happens, my pain will pull me even closer to the Lord.

Suffering has taken me into the throne room of God, where I've had a deeper fellowship with God than I've known at any other time. And as I've identified with Christ's suffering and yielded more fully to Him in my pain, I've drawn even closer.

All of us can find our suffering in Christ's, for there is no suffering our Lord cannot relate to. He knows what it's like to endure sleepless nights and exhausting days, to experience agonizing pain, and to pour Himself out for others who were hostile in return. People used Jesus, flattered Him, criticized

Him, lied about Him, betrayed Him, abandoned Him, mocked Him, humiliated Him, whipped Him, and watched Him die an excruciating death.

If you have ever been betrayed by a friend, someone you loved and trusted, you can know a little of Christ's fellowship in suffering. Or if you have ever begged God to remove your anguish and God denied your desperate request, you can know a little of Christ's fellowship in suffering. Or if you have experienced tormenting, all-consuming physical pain with no relief, you can know a little of Christ's fellowship in suffering.

Barbara Brand knows that fellowship. Her MS and brain lesions cause excruciating pain in her head, so she gets injections into her skull and neck (about forty at a time) just to relieve the agony and nausea. Barbara is part of a PainPal group I'm in with Joni Eareckson Tada, and Barbara has shared how she's drawn nearer to God even in these injections. Barbara says,

> Whenever the needles sink deep into my head, the extreme pain brings into sharp focus Jesus and his crown of thorns. . . . I picture my Savior yielding to the spike-like barbs, wholly embracing his own suffering to rescue me. . . . He is beckoning me into a deeper sanctum of sharing in his sufferings. Wonder of wonders, in some small measure, lowly me gets to identify with and enter *his* grief. The Bible tells me to be an imitator of God, so I get to imitate Jesus and his glad willingness to submit to the Father's

terrible, yet wonderful, will. It's the only way I can, through Christ, do everything. Even these awful injections.[48]

As Barbara has shown me, we can have profound fellowship with Jesus even in the things we most dread. For He draws even closer as we share in His sufferings and breathe in His presence and breathe out His grace.

REFLECT: When has human betrayal given you a taste of what Christ endured? When has emotional or physical suffering given you a taste of what Christ endured?

82

Choosing Gratitude

I will give you thanks with all my heart;
I will sing your praise before the heavenly beings.
PSALM 138:1

I don't like struggling. I want days with little drama, minimal stress, and no pain. But as I look back over my life, I'm most grateful for the days I've had to fight for faith. Through the struggle, my faith has become deeper and richer; I've experienced God's comfort firsthand, and the Bible has come breathtakingly alive.

But I'm usually grateful only in retrospect. It's easiest to appreciate what God has done in my suffering when I am not in the midst of it. But for some trials the pain never passes.

The long-term ongoing struggles that wear on us can be the hardest to give thanks for. Chronic illness. A difficult marriage. A child who is atypical. A disappointing career. Unwanted singleness. Prodigals. Financial worries. Depression. Unfulfilled longings. When we live with these wearisome trials, we often fantasize about how pleasant and normal our lives would be without them.

I've frequently thought, *If I just didn't have to struggle with this one problem, I could handle everything else.* But in reality, this one overarching problem is what is drawing me closest to Jesus.

I'm learning from Joni Eareckson Tada that I can thank God for my suffering, even in the middle of it. She wrote,

> Most of us are able to thank God for His grace, comfort and sustaining power in a trial, but we don't thank Him for the problem, just finding Him in it. . . . Maybe this wheelchair felt like a horrible tragedy in the beginning, but I give God thanks in my wheelchair. . . . I'm grateful for my quadriplegia. It's a bruising of a blessing. A gift wrapped in black. It's the shadowy companion that walks with me daily, pulling and pushing me into the arms of my Saviour. And that's where the joy is. . . .
>
> Your "wheelchair," whatever it is, falls well within the overarching decrees of God. Your hardship and heartache come from His wise and kind hand and for that, you can be grateful. In it and for it.[49]

To be thankful *in* suffering, *for* suffering, is not our natural response. At least, it's not my first response. But God knows our frame and our weaknesses, and He can give us grateful hearts. He can comfort us in ways the world cannot fathom. He can show us the treasures of darkness (Isa. 45:3). I'm learning to ask God to give me a grateful heart and to show me all He's showering on me, rather than feeling guilty when I just want the pain to go away. I can trust He is doing thousands of things for my good even when my gift is wrapped in black.

PRAY: Lord, show me what I can be thankful for in my suffering. I confess that I can only see my problems rather than see Your presence in them. Please give me a grateful heart.

83

The Griefs That Don't Wear Black

In the morning, LORD, you hear my voice;
in the morning I plead my case to
you and watch expectantly.

PSALM 5:3

M y friend calls the hidden sorrows in our lives "the griefs that don't wear black." They aren't visible struggles to others, so people don't grieve with us, bring us a meal, or put us on the church prayer list. Few, if any, know the deep pain we feel.

These sorrows may feel too insignificant to mention, too embarrassing to admit, or too personal to voice. Issues like:

- Children wrestling with their identities and idiosyncrasies.
- Distant spouses who have checked out of the marriage.
- Invisible health problems no one understands.

- Unresolved conflict that keeps us up at night.
- Empty arms that long for a spouse or a baby.
- Depression that has ambushed us for decades.
- Financial struggles that leave us barely paying the bills.
- Relational messes like family secrets, regrets, addictions, and marital failures.

What do we do with these struggles? How do we process all this spoken and unspoken loss and longing?

I start by acknowledging what is painful, recognizing and admitting that my life isn't what I expected it to be. Then I keep pouring my heart out to God, telling Him everything I feel: my sense of injustice and my frustration that God hasn't fixed it, my envy of people who have what my heart desires, and my deep-seated conviction that the Christian life is not supposed to look like this. This isn't a one-and-done, so I plead my case to God every morning.

Then, and generally only then, can I turn to Jesus and start paying attention to His goodness in my life. I get to do life with God. God is taking us all on a journey, one uniquely designed to encounter Him. In my most difficult places, amid my buried dreams and unfulfilled longings, I've seen God most clearly. My faith has been forged in these places.

Some of us who have earnestly prayed for change will not get what we've longed for, as Connally Gilliam reminds us in *And Yet Undaunted*: "Life lived on this fallen planet can and often does stamp a resounding no on our most-longed-for yes."[50] Many of us have experienced that dreaded stamp, and yet in that no we can be assured that God is using that ache for our good. When all we see are empty nurseries, tables for one, and cramped apartments, God is working, doing a thousand things, as He holds us close in these spaces.

So if you have felt the resounding no stamp on your most-longed-for yes, don't think God is indifferent to your pain. Keep turning to God, praying for change, and asking Him to show you His love and goodness *in* this. Keep watching for Him. He will meet you in these longings, and as He does, you'll discover that what He has for you is better than your dreams—it's a life lived with Him.

REFLECT: Where has your life taken a turn from the way you always planned? Take a few minutes to reflect on something that wasn't in the story you would have written about your life. How have these turns impacted your confidence in God's goodness?

84

The Gift of Failure

Then Solomon began to build the house of the
LORD in Jerusalem on Mount Moriah, where
the LORD had appeared to David his father,
at the place that David had appointed, on
the threshing floor of Ornan the Jebusite.

2 CHRONICLES 3:1 ESV

I know what it's like to feel like a failure.

I've scribbled the word *failure* all over my journals. I've wondered if the darkness would ever lift. And I've cried bitter tears through seemingly endless nights.

But I wouldn't trade that time of failure for anything in this world. While I wouldn't want to relive it, the things that I learned through it have been life changing.

I had always defined myself by my accomplishments. First academic success and then success in the business world. After starting a family, I shifted my focus and worked hard to be a supportive wife and mother. I prayed for my husband, homeschooled our daughters, and taught women's Bible studies. It all seemed to be working well. But suddenly everything fell apart.

My husband left me for another woman, citing my inadequacies as a wife. My children walked away from God in anger, highlighting my failure as a parent. Our home became a place of rage and regret, the opposite of the sanctuary it once was.

Everything I had worked for was gone. Everything I had valued disintegrated. Everything that brought me joy was destroyed. Everything but God. In the destruction of those accomplishments that had previously defined me, God touched the deepest places in me. My walk with God was the most real it had ever been. I had no appearances to maintain.

I slowly realized this epic failure was a huge gift. As my life was tested by adversity and failure, I gained a truer sense of who I was. My identity was based solely in Christ.

All of us fail—in big public ways and in small everyday ways—but God uses our failures in remarkable ways when we entrust ourselves to Him.

We see that in the Bible. David sinned against God when he decided to take a census, counting his people instead of counting on God (2 Sam. 24). God punished him, and in David's repentance he built an altar on the threshing floor of Ornan the Jebusite. And on that ground, the place of David's failure and repentance, the temple of the Lord was built.

God's temple in Jerusalem, where He would dwell on earth with man, was built on the ground of human failure. Now God does not dwell in a temple made by human hands. He dwells in us. God's greatest work in us is built on the ground of our failure.

God does His most extraordinary work when we can't rely on ourselves but rely on Him for everything.

———————

WRITE: Pause to review the "failures" in your life, writing them down year by year. Then offer each one to God, and note beside each how God either has redeemed your failure or is leading you, today, to redeem the mistakes you've made.

85

What If Harm Comes to Me?

No harm will come to you;
no plague will come near your tent.

<small>PSALM 91:10</small>

When I first memorized Psalm 91 decades ago, I was excited about the protection God speaks of in it, especially the promise, "No harm will come to you; no plague will come near your tent." Years later, I recited that psalm to Kristi as she fell asleep at night. I assured her that God would protect us, though her dad had left us and our world had disintegrated. Yet as I said those verses aloud, I wondered how they related to us. Harm had come to us, and we felt like one of the ten thousand fallen. I wondered how I should interpret those verses promising protection, deliverance, and provision when I was experiencing the opposite.

I felt a familiar grumbling bubbling up inside of me. Had I not made God my dwelling place? Why did He let us suffer harm? Why hadn't He guarded and delivered us?

I wrote my concerns in my journal. I wanted to know how I was supposed to read this psalm and if I should even pray it. To understand it, I realized I needed to rethink my definition of evil and even of rescue and deliverance. Harm had come to us, but was that the harm God was talking about? As I read and reread the psalm and looked at other Scripture, I recognized that the harm that may come to us has limited effects, effects that apply only to this life. The worst evil, eternal separation from God, will never come near us.

In his last recorded writing, Paul says, "The Lord will rescue me from every evil work and bring me safely into his heavenly kingdom" (2 Tim. 4:18). Paul was beheaded shortly afterwards by Nero, an undeniably evil man, but Paul was rescued in the fullest sense as God brought him safely into his heavenly kingdom.

The end of the psalm says, "When he calls to me, I will answer him; I will be with him in trouble; I will rescue him and honor him" (Ps. 91:15). I realized the Lord has always been with me in trouble and never left. My discouragement came because I wanted him to deliver me out of trouble on my timetable and to answer all my requests with an immediate yes. But I realized that God's presence in trouble has been far better than the absence of trouble without Him.

I now read Psalm 91 with a different perspective. I can abide in the shadow of the Almighty forever. True harm will never come to me. I will never experience the punishment of the wicked. I can be assured He will be with me in trouble. And for all the days ordained for me, the Lord will unfailingly give me what is best until He brings me safely home.

REFLECT: Have you ever felt that God hasn't kept His promises to you? When? Are you feeling that way now?

Incomparable Glory

For our momentary light affliction is producing for us
an absolutely incomparable eternal weight of glory.
2 CORINTHIANS 4:17

As Susan watched her husband die an agonizing death of cancer, she wondered if there was a point to his intense suffering. The hospice workers said they had rarely seen anyone's last days be as torturous and long. Even morphine didn't help the pain. But as Susan studied Scripture, she realized that her husband's faithfulness even in his last hours of life had brought him to an even greater eternal reward. And that changed seemingly meaningless suffering into riches beyond compare, an eternal weight of glory.

Until Susan and I talked, I hadn't considered that our suffering was producing a treasure for us in heaven. I knew all believers would experience spectacular glories in eternity, but a specific reward for faithfulness at first seemed to go against the doctrine of grace. But after delving into the topic and particularly the above verse, I too became convinced, and so thankful, that our suffering is producing glory for us.

Knowing there is a future benefit has given me tremendous comfort thinking of the people I've known who have endured suffering greater than mine. People whose lives have been marked by shattered dreams and relentless pain, with little relief in this life. It thrills me to know they'll receive an extra return for their faithfulness. And in heaven, no one will be jealous of that honor. As Jonathan Edwards said, "It will be no damp to the happiness of those who have lower degrees of happiness and glory, that there are others advanced in glory above them. For all shall be perfectly happy, everyone shall be perfectly satisfied."[51]

Your affliction may not feel light or momentary. Mine certainly has not, as some struggles have dragged on for decades and will likely be with me until I enter glory. But this passage reminds me that they are all light and momentary in relation to eternity. My suffering has an end date and will not last forever, even when it feels interminable. In comparison to eternity, it is momentary. The treasures and glories of heaven will far surpass our pain on earth.

I wonder if part of the reward for persevering through affliction could be a greater capacity for joy. Jesus tells us that the joy of finding the lost coin was greater than the joy of never losing it because restoration brings joy. For everything we've suffered, every loss we've endured, every unfulfilled longing, our joy will be that much deeper when it is restored and fulfilled in heaven.

Those who have experienced God's comfort and protection amid their tears on earth will know a dimension of God that cannot be learned in heaven where there will be no suffering, sorrow, or tears.

Earthly happiness and pleasures fade over time, but the joy of heavenly reward is imperishable and unfading, reserved specifically for us. If you are struggling today, know that your affliction is not meaningless or random. It really is working for your eternal joy. So don't give up now, because endless glory awaits.

———————

MEMORIZE: Write today's verse on an index card. Put it where you'll see it regularly so you can memorize it.

How Can We Possibly Rejoice Always?

Rejoice always, pray constantly, give thanks in
everything; for this is God's will for you in Christ Jesus.
1 THESSALONIANS 5:16–18

As my friend sat in the pre-op room waiting for the nurses to take her mother into surgery, she couldn't stop crying. Her mother's surgery was risky. Everyone knew it. Since the doctors told the family to say goodbye beforehand, she knew this might be the last time she'd see her mother alive.

Sitting by her mother's bed, already grieving, preparing for the worst but hoping for the best, her mother declared, "This is the day the LORD has made; let's rejoice and be glad in it" (Ps. 118:24).

Those words made my friend angry. They were supposed to be comforting, but in that moment they enraged her. *Rejoice? Seriously?!* she thought. That didn't make sense. She couldn't even think of rejoicing right then, especially with all the uncertainty.

Rejoicing was for later, when her mother was in the recovery room and out of danger.

"Don't say that," she hissed. Seeing her mother's pleading smile, she softened and said, "I can't handle the thought of losing you. I can't rejoice. Not now. Not yet. But I will rejoice when you're out of surgery and doing fine."

Her mother then whispered, "Of course you can rejoice. *Rejoice* means 'to return to the source of your joy.' The true source of our joy is Christ, and that will never go away. So I can always rejoice, no matter what I'm going through."

My friend's mother died on the operating table that morning. That bedside encounter was the last time she saw her mother alive.

In the days that followed, she kept replaying her mother's last words. At first it seemed crazy, and moreover impossible, but over time those words have marked her life. Living them has been the best way to honor her mother. And the Lord.

Return to the source of your joy.

What a life-changing perspective on rejoicing. Our joy is not dependent on what happens to us or around us as we are encouraged to "rejoice always, pray constantly, give thanks in everything; for this is God's will for you in Christ Jesus." While we can find joy in the good gifts God has given us—like loving families, deep relationships, healthy bodies, and God-honoring ministries—they cannot be the *source* of our joy.

The source of our joy is the Lord, the Trinity in its fullness. God is the Maker of heaven and earth, who created all the beautiful, wonderful things we enjoy. Jesus is our Redeemer and friend, who has broken the power of sin over us so that we might walk in the newness of life. The Holy Spirit dwells in us—comforting us, guiding us, and guaranteeing us our inheritance. As we fellowship with the Trinity, we need nothing else. *Our joy is complete in the Lord.*

If you are in the middle of a hurricane right now, these words may sound theoretical and empty. But don't discount them. When life is pressing in, return to the source of your joy.

REFLECT: Where is life pressing in on you today? What would it look like for you to return to the source of your joy?

88

Spring Is Coming

*"Arise, my love, my beautiful one, and come
away, for behold, the winter is past; the rain
is over and gone. The flowers appear on the
earth, the time of singing has come, and the
voice of the turtledove is heard in our land."*

SONG OF SONGS 2:10–12 ESV

I pinned the above verse on my bulletin board years ago, unsure
how it even applied to me. I had been reading Song of Songs,
which I often find hard to understand, but those words felt like
they were spoken to me by God Himself.

Life had been excruciating. I had been in the barren season
of winter for years. There was no fruit. No joy. No sunshine.
The skies were darker than they'd ever been, and sunlight rarely
broke through. My daughters were angry, my husband had left
me, my body was failing. Everywhere I turned life felt hopeless. I
felt unwanted, unloved, underappreciated, and overwhelmed all
at the same time.

Yet when I read this verse, I felt the Lord telling me that I was beautiful and beloved, inviting me to draw away with Him. The winter had passed, and the rain had gone. There would soon be singing in the land.

Tears spilled over my Bible. God was speaking to me. I wanted to be beloved and beautiful, but I didn't feel that way. I asked God to show me that I was beloved, confirming this passage was for me.

I told my counselor about this verse and how much encouragement it had brought. I remember her saying without my prompting, "Vaneetha, I feel certain these are God's words for you. Hold onto them."

That corroboration gave me the courage to hold onto hope. Every day I reread the verses, asking God to show me their truth. And as I prayed, I began to see and believe that I was beloved and beautiful, and that change was coming. Though I couldn't see it, I could trust that one day it would come.

Winter dragged on much longer than I thought it would. Yet knowing good lay ahead and that spring was coming gave me hope that God would bring sunshine and fruitfulness in His time.

Years later I remarried, and on our wedding day Joel gave me a plaque engraved with Song of Songs 2:10. He didn't know its meaning to me, which made it even more special. It was a beautiful fulfillment of God's promise, a promise not rooted in Joel but in God.

God has a beautiful future for you. You are His beloved. And one day your winter will be past and gone. Spring will be here. And there will be singing in the land.

PRAY: Lord, You know how dark the skies are right now. Help me remember that this time won't last forever. I trust in You as I'm watching for the morning.

89

Our Days Are in God's Hands

All the days ordained for me were written in
your book before one of them came to be.
PSALM 139:16 NIV

We cannot die one minute before God has ordained it. God knows every one of our days, and we will live every one of them.

We see that principle underscored throughout the pages of Scripture. In 1 Kings 22, King Ahab wants to go into battle against the Syrians, and his usual prophets tell him he will succeed. One lone prophet, Micaiah, warns him that the battle will lead to his death. This prophet goes on to say that Ahab's death was predetermined by God, which is why Ahab was initially enticed to enter the battle.

Ahab doesn't believe the prophet and goes into battle disguised. He believes he can outsmart God, and if people don't know who he is, he will get away. He knows the Syrians were commanded to only fight with the king of Israel, so he feels safe being anonymous. And yet Scripture says, "But a certain man drew his bow at random and struck the king of Israel . . . [and] at evening he died" (1 Kings 22:34–35 ESV).

This act was random on the part of the archer, but his actions were anything but random. His actions accurately fulfilled God's word to the prophet. *And we know that what seems random to us is not random to God, for there is nothing random in all the universe.*

If we believe we can die prematurely, we will often live in fear. What if we make the wrong choice? What if someone else makes the wrong choice? What happens then?

I appreciate one former general's words about his own mortality when he said, "Captain, my religious belief teaches me to feel as safe in battle as in bed. God has fixed the time for my death. I do not concern myself about that, but to be always ready, no matter when it may overtake me. . . . That is the way all men should live, and then all would be equally brave."[52]

A theology that asserts that God is not in control leaves us no security at all. It's unbiblical and unsettling. Do we really want our future to rest in our hands?

God knows when each of us is going to die. All the days ordained for us are written in His book before one of them came to be (Ps. 139:16). We will live out all the days God has purposed for us (Ps. 138:8).

Thankfully we don't worship a God who is helpless but One who spoke the world into existence. God knows when each of us is going to die. We need not fear the day of death, for God Himself will be with us and bring us safely home.

PRACTICE: Write out today's verse: "All the days ordained for me were written in your book before one of them came to be." We need not fear death because our days are in God's hands, not ours. How can that encourage you when you are afraid of the future?

90

Heaven Will Gloriously Overshadow Our Pain

He will wipe away every tear from their eyes. Death will be no more; grief, crying, and pain will be no more, because the previous things have passed away.

REVELATION 21:4

I remember listening to a speaker talk about an inordinately difficult period in her life. Years when she gave up and even stopped praying because nothing seemed to change.

My mind drifted to the people whose lives are just one endless struggle after another. Everyday struggles and life-altering ones. The death of a loved one that leaves a gaping hole in our hearts. Disease that reminds us daily of our mortality. Chronic depression that ambushes us, bringing desperation and inertia. Rebellious children, difficult marriages, divorce, infertility, estrangement, addictions, financial ruin, loneliness, and regret. Some of this pain will never get better. Not in this life.

As I was thinking about this, I felt despair for the millions whose lives are marked by pain. Often my hope rests in the assumption that things will get better. But what if they never do? As I was growing increasingly discouraged, she offered the words that changed everything: "One day, in heaven, all our longings will be met or will fade away."

I exhaled. That's what I needed to hold onto. Heaven will change everything. Things may or may not get better for us in this life, but one day, one glorious day, everything will be made new. One day, in the blink of an eye, we will all be changed. We will have resurrected bodies. Physical bodies, not spirits or disembodied ghosts. There will be no more suffering or death. No sin or regret. No unmet longings. Just endless joy, complete satisfaction, and pleasures forevermore. God created pleasure, and He will maximize it in heaven. Heaven will be incredible because God is incredible.

Everything we love and long for on earth will be in heaven, only better. And it will more than make up for any suffering we've experienced on earth. God has all of eternity to lavish His love and kindness on us where there will be no more crying or pain. Our adventure is just beginning.

C. S. Lewis in *The Last Battle* beautifully describes how we should anticipate heaven:

> For us this is the end of all the stories, and we can most truly say that they all lived happily ever after. But for them it was only the beginning of the real story. All their life in this world

and all their adventures in Narnia had only
been the cover and the title page: now at last
they were beginning Chapter One of the Great
Story which no one on earth has read: which
goes on forever: in which every chapter is better
than the one before.[53]

As Randy Alcorn insightfully reminds us, "'They all lived
happily ever after' is not merely a fairy tale. It's the blood-bought
promise of God for all who trust in the gospel."[54] What an
incredible future awaits.

WRITE: How does knowing that you will live "happily ever
after" impact your outlook on what you are going through? What
encouragement does "happily ever after" give you? Write down
what you want to remember.

Notes

1. Alistair Begg, *CSB Spurgeon Study Bible* (Nashville: Holman Bible Publishers, 2017), 382.

2. Katherine and Jay Wolf, *Suffer Strong* (Grand Rapids, MI: Zondervan, 2020), 65–66.

3. Charles Spurgeon, *Morning and Evening* (Peabody, MA: Hendrickson Publishers, 2021), 461.

4. A. W. Tozer, *The Crucified Life: How to Live Out a Deeper Christian Experience*, ed, James L. Snyder (Minneapolis, MN: Bethany House Publishers, 2011).

5. Jeanne Guyon, *Experiencing the Depths of Jesus Christ* (Nashville, TN: Thomas Nelson, 2000).

6. Laura Story and Shelly Esser, "Mercies in Disguise," *Just between Us* (July 11, 2023), https://justbetweenus.org/everyday-faith/exclusive-interviews/mercies-in-disguise.

7. Daniel Gilbert, "What You Don't Know Makes You Nervous," *New York Times*, May 21, 2009, https://archive.nytimes.com/opinionator.blogs.nytimes.com/2009/05/20/what-you-dont-know-makes-you-nervous/.

8. Edward T. Welch, *Running Scared: Fear, Worry, and the God of Rest* (Greensboro, NC: New Growth Press, 2007), 144–45.

9. Evelyn Christenson, *What Happens When Women Pray* (Wheaton, IL: Victor Books, 1991), 89–90.

10. John Piper, "God Is Always Doing 10,000 Things in Your Life," Desiring God, January 1, 2013, https://www.desiringgod.org/articles/god-is-always-doing-10000-things-in-your-life.

11. Paul Miller, *A Praying Life* (Colorado Springs, CO: NavPress, 2009), 203.

12. Samuel Rutherford, *The Loveliness of Christ* (Carlisle, PA: Banner of Truth Trust, 2007), 2.

13. Mother Frances Dominica, *Prayer* (Amate Press,1981), as quoted by Rueben Job, *A Guide to Prayer for Ministers and Other Servants* (Nashville: Upper Room, 1983), 16.

14. Zacharias Ursinus, "Question 1," *Heidelberg Catechism*, Westminster Theological Seminary, accessed October 5, 2024, https://students.wts.edu/resources/creeds/heidelberg.html.

15. Ursinus, *Heidelberg Catechism*.

16. Larry Crabb, *Conversations Journal: A Forum for Authentic Transformation* (Kettering, OH: Fall/Winter 2011), 25.

17. Timothy Keller, *Prodigal God* (New York, NY: Penguin, 2008), 39.

18. Clint Watkins, *Just Be Honest* (London, UK: The Good Book Company, 2024), 73.

19. Hope Blanton and Christine Gordon, *Lamentations: At His Feet Studies* (Omaha, NE: 19Baskets, 2023), 41, 53, 64, 75, 87.

20. Tish Harrison Warren, *Prayer in the Night* (Downers Grove, IL: InterVarsity Press, 2021), 41.

21. Alexander McLaren, "Anxious Care," *Sermons Preached in Union Chapel, Manchester* (Manchester: Dunnill, Palmer, and Company, 1859), 288, https://quoteinvestigator.com/2021/07/03/anxiety/#f+439865+1+2, accessed October 6, 2024.

22. Charles H. Spurgeon, "The Simplicity and Sublimity of Salvation," sermon delivered March 6, 1890, at Metropolitan Tabernacle, The Spurgeon Center, https://www.spurgeon.org/resource-library/sermons/the-simplicity-and-sublimity-of-salvation/#flipbook.

23. Elisabeth Elliot, *Be Still My Soul* (Ann Arbor, MI: Servant Publications, 2003), 34.

24. Cameron Cole, *Heavenward* (Wheaton, IL: Crossway, 2024), 26.

25. Elisabeth Elliot, *These Strange Ashes* (Grand Rapids, MI: Revell, 1998), 11.

26. Joni Eareckson Tada, "The Stakes Are Higher Than You Think," *Revive Our Hearts* podcast, November 15, 2013, https://www.reviveour hearts.com/podcast/revive-our-hearts/stakes-are-higher-you-think.

27. Joseph Bayly, *View from a Hearse* (Bloomington, IN: Warhorn, 2014), Kindle loc. 488.

28. Paul David Tripp, *Suffering: Gospel Hope When Life Doesn't Make Sense* (Wheaton, IL: Crossway, 2018), 24.

29. John Piper, *Future Grace* (Colorado Springs, CO: Multnomah Books, 2005), 10.

30. Attributed to Phillips Brooks, Good Reads, https://www.good reads.com/quotes/10581955-i-do-not-pray-for-a-lighter-load-but-for, accessed October 7, 2024.

31. Samuel Rutherford, *The Loveliness of Christ* (Carlisle, PA: Banner of Truth Trust, 2007), 64.

32. John Newton as quoted by Timothy Keller, *Walking with God through Pain and Suffering* (New York, NY: Penguin, 2013), 266.

33. Thomas O. Chisholm, "Great Is Thy Faithfulness," 1923, public domain.

34. Matthew Henry, George Whitefield, and Alexander MacLaren, *Classic Sermon Outlines* (Peabody, MA: Hendrickson, 2001).

35. Amy Carmichael, *Made in the Pans* (Edinburgh, UK: Oliphants, 1918), 99–100.

36. This is from a letter to Elisabeth Elliot's parents after her husband Jim was murdered in 1956.

37. Elliot, *Be Still My Soul*, 32.

38. Mother Teresa, as quoted by Richard Stearns, *Lead Like It Matters to God* (Downers Grove, IL: InterVarsity, 2021), 3–4.

39. Douglas Kaine McKelvey, *Every Moment Holy* (Nashville: Rabbit Room Press, 2017), 201.

40. McKelvey, *Every Moment Holy*, 204–5.

41. Ted Wueste, *Trusting God in the Wilderness* (Phoenix: Desert Direction, 2021), 39.

42. David Martyn Lloyd-Jones, *Spiritual Depression* (Grand Rapids, MI: Eerdmans, 1965), 20.

43. Mark Vroegop, "Dare to Hope in God: How to Lament Well," *Desiring God*, April 6, 2019, https://www.desiringgod.org/articles/dare-to-hope-in-god.

44. Miriam Huffman Rockness, *A Blossom in the Desert* (Grand Rapids, MI: Discovery, 2007), 147.

45. John Piper, Twitter, March 1, 2016, https://twitter.com/John Piper/status/704653441533132800?lang=en.

46. Edward T. Welch, *A Small Book for the Anxious Heart* (Greensboro, NC: New Growth Press, 2019), 98, 107.

47. Wueste, *Trusting God in the Wilderness*, 17.

48. Joni Eareckson Tada, *Songs of Suffering* (Wheaton, IL: Crossway, 2022), 115.

49. Joni Eareckson Tada, foreword, in Nancy Leigh DeMoss book, *Choosing Gratitude* (Chicago: Moody, 2009), 12–13.

50. Paula Rinehart and Connolly Gillam, *And Yet Undaunted* (Colorado Springs, CO: NavPress, 2019), 48.

51. Jonathan Edwards, *The Works of Jonathan Edwards, A.M., Vol. 2* (London, UK: William Ball, 1839), 902.

52. George Francis Robert Henderson, *Stonewall Jackson and the American Civil War* (London: Longmans, Green, 1902), 200.

53. C. S. Lewis, *The Last Battle* (New York: HarperCollins, 1984), 228.

54. Gavin Ortland, "Looking Forward to a Heaven We Can Imagine—an Interview with Randy Alcorn," The Gospel Coalition, March 9, 2015, https://www.thegospelcoalition.org/article/looking-forward-to-a-heaven-we-can-imagine.